The Western Way

Lawrence Johns

Published by Conscious Publishing, 2023.

THE WESTERN WAY

First edition. February 3, 2023.

Copyright © 2023 Lawrence Johns.

ISBN: 978-1929096060

Written by Lawrence Johns.

Table of Contents

for C H J

The Eastern Way

Before you achieve Enlightenment

In the Western Way

Before you activate Future Earth

And explore the alluring planets

Of Deep fleeing Space

You must become Enlightened

In the Eastern Way

Many philosophies arise in the East

But only the Realization of Hui Neng

Is accurate and powerful enough

To serve our present purpose

As a young man he overheard

A line from the Diamond Sutra

And instantly understood

The Emptiness of Consciousness

Suddenly recognized

The total Nothingness of Self

When you experience the Void

You enter the camp of Buddha

And what you learn there

Will influence all future Action

As you master the techniques

Of Chan Meditation

Everything you know

As the Real World

And the Self

Becomes radical Un-Knowing

My Sagaxi

Sit comfortably

Eyes closed

And bring it down

To four breaths a minute

Now you can attend the demands

Of five thousand Thoughts

Racing and jostling your Mind

The innocuous white noise

Of anticipated Events

The involuntarily tripped synapses

Of a properly functioning Body

And the crowd of clamoring Emotions

Seeking immediate approval

Are quickly subtracted

From the flow of Consciousness

By a quick flare of inattention

But those intimately connected

To your historical sense of Self

Run fierce in your Blood

And require a metaphor

Imagine Emptiness is the Sky

And each Idea carrying your Self

Into the next minute a white cloud

Crossing that bright blue arc

Fading from view they call out

Claiming to be your progeny

But they're not yours

And they're not You

Because your Self has become Void

What remains when all Thoughts

Vanish from the Mind

Is the Pure Consciousness

Of Hui Neng

All is Buddha Nature

All is Vigilance

Wisdom is Meditation

And Meditation is everything you do

My Sagaxi

Buddha is our first worthy Opponent

Our duel with the Void

Provides major Resistance to the Will

We modify Chan teachings

To strengthen the Western Individual

Once you've experienced your Self

As Non-Being in Chan Meditation

The Vigilance you learn in the East

Will be of great service

When you practice Voletic Meditation

And meet the complex and myriad Dangers

Awaiting you on the Western Way

Non-Being

―――

Buddha's Genius crushed

The Hindu tradition

Of Karma and Reincarnation

That believed in recurring cycles

Of intense and constant Suffering

His hypersensitivity

To the mental and physical Pain

Of the millions born into Hindu Faith

Inspired him to invent a lasting cure

If the Self as Being is doomed

To suffer frustration of all Desire

Then You must go back

Before Self and Being

Before your mother was born

Back to Non-Being

Where there's no Self to suffer

Liberation from the grinding wheel

Of Karma can be found

In the Meditation Experience

6

Bodhidarma brought this message

To a Taoist China compatible

With esoteric Buddhist Philosophy

Hui Neng's analysis

Of Pure Consciousness

Made Realization instantaneous

If all Being is Non-Being

There's no Attainment

There's no Nirvana

You're Buddha Here and Now

To Western Philosophy heavily influenced

By logic and linguistics

Liberation from Reincarnation

Has little significance or Meaning

But since Parmenides the question of Being

Has perplexed the Western Mind

Heidegger stunned a Modernity

Comfortably geared to minimize ontology

When he asked

Why is there Something instead of Nothing?

Parmenides claimed Non-Being

Logically cannot Be

But in Voletic Meditation

When You entered Non-Being

Enveloped by Blackness

Within and Without

You found the answer to Heidegger

You had no eyes or Brain

To process No-Information

You felt the vast expanse

Of Nothingness as Consciousness

The Gravity was monstrous

And your space horribly small

Compacted beyond measure

By the increasing pressure of Non-Being

Time was agonizingly slow

Waiting for something to happen

Waiting a minute longer

Then You understood this slim minute

Had just repeated itself

A million billion times

This Void was so monotonous

This Non-Being so oppressive

That You raised the Will To Be

8

And burst into Being

Schopenhauer

The young Schopenhauer

Conceived of the World

As Will and Representation

He was unconcerned with its genesis

In Non-Being

Unacquainted with the principles

And overflow of Evolution

Like Buddha he was distressed

By the Suffering of Man

But unable to propose a solution

To Schopenhauer every individual Being

Was a helpless ignorant victim

Of the Will To Live

From bacteria to sequoias

From fire ants to distant Galaxies

Everything and everyone that exists

Is conditioned by Will

To survive at all costs

So inevitably the History of Man

Is constant bloody warfare

Domination and Deceit

Misery always and everywhere

There's no way out

Because Will is both

The Thing In Itself

The Un-Knowable One

And every individuated Self

Identical with that One

Representations of the World

In Sensations

Emotions

And Ideas

Are a sequence of deceptions

Reporting to the blind Will

Schopenhauer habitually escapes

This brutal Will To Live

By contemplating Fine Art

Attending the Frankfurt Opera

And hiking in the Black Forest

Where he loses his bitter Self

For a benign parenthetical moment

In the exquisite beauties of Nature

To Schopenhauer all empirical evidence

Supports a pessimistic Philosophy of Life

He champions the celibate monk

He applauds the ascetic in his cold cave

Attempting to deny the Will

By repudiating sex

And never eating for pleasure

He claims the highest Goal of Man

Is to negate the Will To Live

In every possible way

My Sagaxi

Schopenhauer's invention of Will

Overshadows his systemic Pessimism

And curious affection for saints

Will is the necessary ground

For all Modern Philosophy

That takes Life seriously

The problem with Schopenhauer

Is Passivity

He views the World

As a contemptuous spectator

Of the spooked stumbling masses

Doomed to repetitions of Disaster

Without Understanding or recourse

He's too entranced

By Kant's moral Idealism

To appreciate or inspire the Talent

Of the Extraordinary Individual

To fashion a Reality

That suits his current Fancy

Now that you've experienced

The explosive Transition

From Non-Being to Being

Your growing Confidence

Is the engine to Higher Ambitions

The Western Way defeats Suffering

By raising Third Will Intelligence

Maximizing the Self

And affirming the Tragedy of Life

My Sagaxi

In the theater of Dionysus

Where Aeschylus and Sophocles

Enacted the bizarre crimes

Of their mythic ancestors

And elevated horror narratives

Of Misfortune and Misunderstanding

To poetic Ecstasies

Apollonian healing occurred

In scheduled festival cycles

And continues to soothe

The Western Mind today

The Eastern Way needs

Liberation and Salvation

But the West is fine with Mystery

And the periodic literary catharsis

That strips accreted carbon

From blocked cylinders

Of overworked Self-Consciousness

Now that you've willed your Self

Back from the Void

You understand the Value

Of conceiving Being as Action

And why Schopenhauer

As the passive Observer

And harsh critic of Life

14

Is our second worthy Opponent

The Next Men

———

The blade of grass

Crashing up through the sidewalk

The billion species

Of Flora and Fauna

Desperately hunting food

To survive their next survival

In the bubbling black cauldron

Of ferocious bacteria and viruses

Mutating fast to kill them

The baby seeking the nipple

Fearing with every sharp breath

To be totally forgotten

And robbed of Life

Are daily reminders

That our sense impressions

Of the Real World

And the whirling circus of mental images

Derived from those recordings

Are functional Illusions

Created by the Mind

To ease the Struggle for Life

And give it personal Value

Lovers aren't concerned

With the Truth of their Beloved

Love is the Fiction

That flees strangling Tedium

Their romantic Madness

Recognizes no analysis or rational counsel

In Shakespearean thrall to simile

They release to sweet spirals of orgasm

Momentarily and blissfully ignorant

Of the dark machinations

Of social and political Intent

Hovering like vultures in the perfumed air

My Sagaxi

The religious and political cults

Of the New Medieval

Hyperbolized by high technology

And fueled by endemic stupidity

Recognize no reason

In their clash of belief systems

Everything is demonizing

Everything is vulgar solicitation

Of righteous Anger

And murderous Hate

Every Vice is a Virtue

And every Monstrosity a Beauty

These decadent revaluations

And comprehensive reversals

Of Western Culture

Mask a great Sorrow

Homosapiens are dying

After three hundred thousand years

Homosapiens are dying

And want to take the World

Down into Non-Being with them

The Sapiens death rattle

Echoing in contagious paranoia

Spontaneous violence

And traumatic divorce from Nature

Is the dark dissonant Herald

Of your timely Evolutionary Leap

From Sapiens to Sagax

My Sagaxi

You're the Next Men

You're the necessary refutation

Of contemporary Nihilism

And politically orchestrated Fear

Yes

Sapiens had sporadic Genius

But in the end

They overdosed on Greed

Perversion

And bloody tribal Revenge

In the Dying Time of Sapiens

You're restarting the Party of Man

You're the surprise Guest

Arriving without invitation

Jumping the Evolutionary Line

To control Future Earth

Three Will Theory

―――

With Nietzsche whispering in my ear

During the biggest mistakes

And trickiest revisions

I first introduced Three Will Theory

In my epic poem Beyond Exile

And over the next thirteen years

It became a defining lens

For the apperception of the World

As new philosophical insight

And scientific evidence arose

What Schopenhauer and Nietzsche

Had conceived as a Unity

Determining Cosmic and Human Events

Under close investigation

Is the result of Three distinct Wills

Competing for control of Reality

Because they appeared sequentially

I called them First Will

Second Will

And Third Will

Three Will Theory describes

The Fundamental Forces

That move the World

Manifest in their Histories

Interactions

And Goals

First Will is the Will To Be

The Creative Force

And its cognates

The desire for Power

The desire for Life

The desire for Play

The desire for Pleasure

The desire for Love

The desire for Order

The desire for Virtue

The desire for Composition

The desire for Construction

The desire for Repair

The desire for Maintenance

The desire for Adventure

The desire for Legacy

The desire for Progeny

The desire for Continuation

First Will is the Imperative

Of Being to Stay In Being

In its primary Identity

First Will is reproductive Nature

Delivering endless seeds and sperm

To every square inch of Earth

And the billion trillion planets

Out There

It's the relentless Drive

That keeps all forms of Life

Hunting

Multiplying

And racing on

First Will is Conscious

But not Self-Aware

It instinctively adapts to Danger

And changing environmental Conditions

But lacks the ability

To make the correct Decision

From a host of possibilities

As First Will moves through Spacetime

At some clearly inevitable

But often surreal and shocking point

It experiences Fatigue

The cold grip of Meaninglessness

And the tremendous pressure

To Give It All Up

When First Will hits the Wall

It recoils and becomes Second Will

The Will to Not-Be

Driving to Self-Annihilation and Death

Second Will is also Conscious

And not Self-Aware

In its primary Identity

Second Will is devastating Nature

Grinding every great Idea into Idiocy

Every Bloom into Dust

And every Pleasure into Pain

Second Will is the Destructive Force

And its cognates

The desire for Power

The desire for Death

The desire for Hate

The desire for Faith

The desire for Disease

The desire for Suffering

The desire for Madness

The desire for Decay

The desire for Pain

The desire for Repetition

The desire for Addiction

The desire for Depression

The desire for Torture

The desire for Perversion

The desire for Disorder

The desire for Deconstruction

The desire for Reversal

Of everything First Will

Ever initiated or invented

Second Will has the Lust

To annihilate all Spacetime

By killing Man's Confidence

In his Space and his Time

When Second Will hits the Wall

Of Non-Being

It recoils and becomes First Will again

This Reaction Event

Is the central Paradox

In the History of Consciousness

And the cause and cradle

Of Man's Self-Awareness

Without the destroying force of Second Will

We would be frolicking oceans

With the dolphins

Or reaching for purple fruit

With silverback apes in the jungle

Without the deep examination of Existence

Sparked by confrontation with Non-Being

We would not Know who we Are

My Sagaxi

First Will and Second Will

Are causally embraced

In a tango of Positive-Negative

Action-Reaction

And Life-Death

On cosmic scales the Struggle

Between First and Second Will

Maintains the Equilibrium

Of all Physical Events

First Will produces the gas

That condenses into new stars

And Second Will blasts their cores

Into supernovae when they starve

Ejecting heavy elements and dust

That First Will slowly turns into planets

And rich new possibilities of Life

Emerging from their deep azure oceans

On the stage of Man's mendacious History

Second Will Self-Annihilations

Cause the Wars

Insanity

And Decadence

Periodically destroying Civilizations

And sabotaging all Higher Ambitions

It stimulates the strange pleasure of Sapiens

When they witness other Sapiens in pain

It causes every homicide

Suicide

And government policy

That accelerates nuclear fears

Climate catastrophe

And global famine

Second Will champions Chaos

Bad habits and bad choices

In everything and everyone

Angrily deconstructing

And systematically corrupting

Every hierarchic form of Order

Created and maintained by First Will

These heavy Second Will assaults

Have dominated Western Culture

For millennia

But First Will always Wins Out

Overcoming the slaughter

Stupidity

And cowardice of Sapiens

To create new and better Opportunities

For Life to Thrive

My Sagaxi

Third Will emerges prodigiously powerful

And existentially transcendent

From the Struggle

Between First and Second Will

Third Will is the Will To Intelligence

The Force of Improvement

The desire to synthesize Future and Past

Into a Present of Higher Value

And transform slow Evolutionary Motion

Into lightning Decisions by the Advanced Mind

That produce a Superior Reality

Third Will is Conscious and Self-Aware

The Desire for Intellectual Solutions

And their cognates

The desire for Power

The desire for Wisdom

The desire for Knowledge

The desire for Higher Consciousness

The desire for Higher Self-Awareness

The desire for Reason

The desire for Innovation

The desire for Control

The desire for Philosophy

The desire for Science

The desire for Technology

The desire for Experimentation

The desire for Invention

The desire for Synthesis

The desire for Simulation

The desire for Analysis

The desire for Manipulation

The desire for Strategy

The desire for Tactics

The desire for Imagination

The desire for Understanding

The desire for Logic

The desire for Deception

The desire for Advantage

The desire for Narrative

The desire for Competition

The desire for Cooperation

The desire for Personality

When aligned with First Will

Third Will is Intelligent Life

Constantly acquiring Knowledge

That supports and directs new Decisions

It's the Momentum

Of philosophical and aesthetic Genius

Carried by Extraordinary Individuals

From the Past of Western Culture

To a Future of Higher Mental Powers

When aligned with Second Will

In the New Medieval

Third Will is Intelligent Death

Sabotaging and perverting

Every instance of First Will Imperative

And promoting the Virtues of Decadence

With scientifically crafted propaganda

That manipulates Nation States

Into monumental Lies and barbarous Wars

In the Dying Time of Sapiens

It projects an Artificial World

Claiming electronic guidance of Society

A vulgar hologram posing as Flesh

A vetted broadcast of Misinformation

Falsely analyzed by mimes

And enthusiastically received

By a global audience of cretins and fools

In the Dying Time of Sapiens

It publishes mind control commands

On internet podcasts and YouTube videos

Inciting random violence by sleepers

To accelerate the daily Terror and Chaos

My Sagaxi

In its search for logical and lasting Solutions

The hyperrationality of Third Will

Can be heavily influenced

And occasionally overwhelmed

By strong emotional Oscillations

Flowing from its Interactions

With First and Second Will

It can accelerate bold Creation today

Then merciless Destruction tomorrow

Or both Wills simultaneously

When Conditions are confused

My Sagaxi

The World is Three Wills

And their Interpretations

All Three Wills have intense Desire for Power

All Three are Moving the World

In Present Time

What we witness as Change

Is the complicated shifting alliance

Of First and Third Will

Fighting the Second and Third

For control of the Real World

And its most powerful Interpretations

Three Will Theory reflects

The Indo-European affection for triads

And the Hegelian history of Ideas

When the Three Wills evolve

With the calm majesty of the Seasons

Or the intense torrent of Thought

The Force of First Will produces Birth

With the biological and mental functions

That develop young Life

The Force of Second Will induces Death

With the matrix of functions that destroy old Life

The Force of Third Will excites Understanding

With theoretical and practical Solutions

To the perennial Battle

Between First and Second Will

My Sagaxi

Quantum Field Theory provides a model

For the tremendous kinetic Energy

Of Will in the World and Will in the Self

When every point in Space

And every moment in Time is connected

What Modern Physics once assumed

Were solid proton and neutron balls

Sitting stationary in a nucleus

Surrounded by circling electrons

Is now pictured in the Standard Model

As three Up and Down Quarks

Bound by strong force Gluons

Pulsating in a cloud of electron probability

The Spin generated

On the Quarks by the Gluons

At the speed of light

Gives the nucleus its Energy and Mass

Analogously

The tremendous Spin

Generated by the Three Wills

Battling each other

Faster than the speed of light

Creates sufficient Voletic Energy

To carry the Arrow of Time forward

Accelerate the expansion of the Universe

And convert into the Voletic Mass

That protects Galaxies and Filaments

From random collisions and decay

My Sagaxi

Despite many stupendous discoveries

That have refined our perception

Of the visible Universe

The reductionism of modern physicists

That ignores Will and Mind

In theories based on pure mathematics

Has forced them into systemic failure

Searching for a particle to prove

Their Dark Energy and Dark Matter conjectures

And the unsolvable infinities that arise

When attempting to unify

Quantum Field Theory and Gravity

Despite its outstanding technology

And fascinating speculations

Modern Physics can explain

Less than 5% of Reality

And nothing of its Goals

By integrating Will and Mind

With empirical evidence

Three Will Theory describes

How Will moves the World

How Man understands that Motion

And how the Advanced Mind

Constructs its Goals

My Sagaxi -

The Struggle of Three Wills in the World

Is consistent and resonant

With the Struggle of Three Wills

Inside the Self

When you can identify your internal state

And match it to actual Conditions

Every tactical move and winning strategy

Looks easy

Inevitable

And warm

Like the Sun rising in the East

The V Dome

———

The discovery of Voletic Energy

Immediately created problems

With its accurate measurement

And highest practical use

After two years of false starts

And dead ends

The breakthrough occurred

After studying Nick Nelson's

Experiments with natural vortexes

That revealed a small Spacetime anomaly

I found that Voletic Energy

Is more subtle and fundamental than Gravity

And impossible to detect

With electromagnetic measuring devices

The Voletic Quantum Field

Extends throughout the Universe

And interacts with every physical and mental Event

After applying the Copenhagen Interpretation

Of the quantum wave function

It became clear that observation

Of the Voletic Wave by the Human Mind

Was the only way it collapsed into a particle

I came to call the voletron

Like electrons and other particles

Voletrons are interconnected

Everywhere in the Voletic Field

Information given one voletron

Is simultaneously received

By all other voletrons in Spacetime

My Sagaxi

Working with this electron simile

I eventually had a table model

Of a V Dome device that produced

An infinite Spacetime anomaly

Throughout the Voletic Quantum Field

With intriguing potential

For improved Powers of Mind

And access to New Information

I began a controlled series of tests

With friends and volunteers

That produced frustrating results

Until I realized the V Dome

Was more than a receiver

Or simple voletron trap

It functioned like an amplifier

That boosted the Voletic Field

To a detectable level

And also like a transceiver

Able to send and receive Information

Throughout the Universe

However

It was soon apparent

That only Advanced Minds

Could observe or influence the Field

Weak

Caged

Or heavily conditioned Minds

Handicapped by Faith and other baggage

Imported their hardwired agendas

And psychoses into the experiment

Or had no Experience at all

Some tried banal mindfulness

Paranormal channeling

Or traditional religious prayer

To excite the Voletic Field

Without a hint of success

Some tried using the V Dome

For stock market investments

Sex magic

And New Age trysts

With angels and demons

So I stopped the tests

And withdrew the V Dome

Permanently from public view

Determined to reserve it

As a prototype of future technology

For those Few well on the Way

To Western Enlightenment

To refresh my technique

I recalled my student days

In Hong Kong with S L Yen

And modified Chan Meditation

To fit our present purpose

In Voletic Meditation

I could contact Other Intelligences

And explore Other Planets

I saw the Universe

As the Choice of all Possibilities

Acting at every distance

From every starting point

And every frame of reference

In a superposition of Time and No-Time

I was in multiple places at once

Sitting comfortably at 65 degrees

In my living room

And simultaneously investigating

The stunning Landscapes

And intricate Communications

Of Deep singing Space

My Sagaxi

The New Information acquired

In your Explorations

Will come from confrontations

With physical and psychological Obstacles

Man has never met before

Document these Challenges well

Because every successful Solution

42

To this High Strangeness and Deep Resistance

Boosts your High Intelligence

And strengthens your Personality

The Task

———

The contemporary hegemony

Of Second and Third Will

Over Modern American Society

Is so complete and insidious

That Dying Sapiens turn cannibal

Like overcrowded manic rats

And submit to rampaging Hysteria

With a false and vapid smile

In the grotesque encore

Of Medieval Wars and Plague

The Western Values of Individuality

Freedom

And Privacy

Are revalued by groupthink

And the Eastern hive mentality

That only sanctions Personal Identity

Within a social and economic consensus

Of productive despotic mediocrity

In the decomposing New Medieval

All the guiding Virtues First Will produced

To build and maintain Western Culture

Are systematically deconstructed

And subjected to humiliating public apology

In a Second Will political meme stream

Started by the Chinese Cultural Revolution

My Sagaxi

Homosapiens are mutating so quickly

In their Death Spiral

That transhumanism is no longer

An engineering Romance

Or science fiction extrapolation

The Commerce Class is advertising

The Homoborg

As the New Efficiency

As the New Popularity

The eyes of Sapiens Youth

Have developed double reptilian flaps

From screen glare

Long thumbs for better texting

And necks permanently crooked

From checking notifications

On their smartphones

Like vampires they avoid mirrors

Because they're repulsed

By the consistent lack of reflection

But they can recapture Affection

And gain six figures of followers

By accepting a miniature Chip

Drilled into their skulls

Connected to the cloud

They can outperform their colleagues

Connected to the cloud

They can watch everything

Everybody is doing everywhere

Connected to the cloud

American Youth

Is the last Self- Deception

Of the Last Men

And a major battlefield success

Of Second and Third Will

Over the First and Third

My Sagaxi

The Commerce Class

Has programmed the Homoborg

With its own recurring Nightmares

A Remington painting of a buffalo herd

Under howling attack by a wolfpack

A cartoon sketch of a foaming London crowd

Watching a debtor hang in the public square

Falsified emails demanding personal passwords

To retrieve a hacked birth certificate

Without our intervention

A chipped Totalitarian America

Is the last barbaric move

In the endgame of Western Civilization

Our momentous and immediate Task

Is to terminate the New Medieval

Restore the Wisdom Class to Power

And immediately take the Homoborgs

Under our Wing

The Restoration

———

The classical Greeks revered

The Wisdom of the Seven Sages

Retained in stunning fragments

From the mist of their prehistory

Plato invented the term Philosophy

To express his admiration

For the early Greek Thinkers

In the colonies of Ionia and Italy

That extended the Genius of The Seven

Into a speculative literature of Ideas

He showcases the dialectic blade

Of Socrates in keen ethical dialogs

But Plato is at his best

When transmitting and extending

The original Ideas of Pythagoras

Parmenides

And Heraclitus

That sparked Western Thought

Disgusted by the fatal Rhetoric

Of Athenian democracy

And education based solely on Homer

Plato wrote The Republic

To present a new literary model

Of the Perfect City State

He proposed to end

The constant intermural bloodshed

Between the oligarchs

Democrats

And tyrants in Athens

By returning to the Golden Age

Of the Philosopher King

His idea of authentic political Power

Grounded in the mastery of music

Mathematics

And Philosophy

Found no favor

In the raucous city of Persuasion

And crowd-pleasing Flattery

Famously protected by Athena

The armored Goddess of Wisdom

So Plato sailed to Syracuse

To teach the Tyrants

Dionysus II and Dion

What Athenian democracy

Had contemptuously declined

Unsurprisingly

The tutorials intended to produce

A living Philosopher King

On the model of the Seven Sages

Were delayed

Derided

And eventually the accumulation

Of minor palace blunders

Dispatched Plato to the slave market

At Aegina

Where he was bought and rescued

By Anniceris

A former student from Cyrene

After the Syracuse debacle

Plato never advocated the Philosopher King

Or the Perfect City State again

As he aged Egyptian in The Laws

Dismissive of the Sensory World

And bitterly detached

From the erotic Poetry of his Youth

My Sagaxi

In rascally obscure and carefully veiled Satire

Thomas More revisited Plato's concept

Of the Perfect City State

In his provocative Utopia

Dressed in Medieval robes

And playing loose with Socialist themes

His literal Latin No-Where

Placed on a large temperate island

At the Edge of the World

Banished private property

Installed rule by Philosophers

And provided free food and housing

For all Four Classes of Society

As a literary fantasy More's Utopia

Displays many acute psychological insights

Particularly his prophesy

Easily spotted behind and between the lines

That nothing like Utopia could ever happen

In the Real World

And any deviation from the Christian Credo

Would be immediately and cruelly punished

With the rise of Communism

In Russia and China

More's vision of social Equality

Cynically enforced by theological Terror

Was fattened and devoured

By Eastern Police Totalitarianism

With brushstrokes like scalpel cuts

George Orwell portrayed the Big Lies

Surveillance

And dehumanization

Required by Eastern Communist States

To run their sadistic and highly effective

Third Will Simulations of Utopia

And soon the Consciousness of Dystopia

Became a High Concern in Western Culture

As the Existential Anxiety

Exposed by Sartre and Camus

Weakened the Spine of the Western Mind

My Sagaxi

Two millennia before Plato

The Derwids were the Wisdom Class

That ruled and maintained Western Culture

They made the Major Decisions

And guided the Four Classes

Towards secure and satisfying Futures

After twenty years of training

A Derwid was the Leader

Judge

Doctor

Scholar

Poet

Philosopher

Counselor

Astronomer

Herbalist

And General Authority

For everyone in the village

He embodied Civic Virtue

In his public Decisions and Actions

He advised the Noble Class

Where to build their homes

And when to engage their Enemies

He counseled the Commerce Class

On new products and trading routes

He informed the Working Class

Of new tools and crop rotations

Respect for the Wisdom of the Derwids

Was the Bond keeping Ancient Western Culture

Strong and united through the millennia

As it spread from the Danube valley

To distant Dublin and Madras

My Sagaxi

At some point during the incessant wars

With the early Roman Empire

The ruling Power of the Derwids

Was usurped by the Noble Class

And its eventual fusion

With the egalitarian Dogma

Of missionary Christianity

The Derwids adapted

Assimilated

Or went underground

Into European secret orders and societies

The Industrial Revolution and rapid ascent

To unchecked political Power

By the Commerce Class

In the Nineteenth Century

Reduced the Derwids

To quaint folk tales and caricatures

Penned by British Celtic revivalists

And simplistically retold today

In popular TV series and video games

My Sagaxi

Contemporary educational systems

In both Capitalist and Communist Societies

Have effectively extinguished Respect

For the Wisdom and Noble Classes

And the Working Class

Has consequently become fat passive prey

For the targeted electronic brainwashing

Of savvy commercial and political Predation

After two millennia

Subservient to kings

Priests

And dissembling ministers

The global operating system

Of the dominant Commerce Class

Has become an effective weapon

Of Mind and Behavior Control

And enjoys sweet Revenge

Whenever it induces a member

Of the Wisdom and Noble Classes

To translate his natural Love of Family

Into Adoration of the Corporate State

The American version of the system

Exults with special Pleasure

Whenever a Free Individual undresses his Pride

And slips naked into the fetid steams of profit

My Sagaxi

Freud would consider it the Return

Of a long-repressed Commerce Class

And the final Discontent of Western Civilization

With the Commerce Class in Power

The Honor that defined the Actions

And Metaphorical Sense of Being

Of the two higher Classes

Is systematically corrupted

Ridiculed in the marketplace

And replaced by a Literal Sense of Being

That makes everyone a mad customer

Eager to exert the Power of Destruction

In this disturbing Discontent

Professors are schooled by their students

To submit to the business and political ideologies

That guarantee good grades and job prospects

Professionals must compete with bloated bills

To deal with ravenous insurance companies

And every teenager dreams of becoming

A billionaire influencer on Instagram

By promoting fashion accessories

And posting scandalous photos of the Stars

In this coopted Discontent

Journalists knows that Truth

Is synonymous with the highest number of clicks

And contemporary philosophers compete to validate

Big Tech's disingenuous ethical altruism

The commercial operating system

Has become so successful

That in the New Medieval

American Intelligence

Has degenerated into the disgrace

Of looking for the best deal

On everything and everybody

All the time

My Sagax

In the TV series I'm Carlos Now

I worked with hypertalented Paul Flum

Writing and filming the best strategy

To overthrow the Commerce Class

Our screenplay of Improvisations

And Juxtapositions

Based on Original Myths

Poetry

And Comedy

Successfully spiked the insatiable Greed

Of the Commerce Class

And accelerated its Second Will Death-Wish

Without any reference to Revolution

Or mob-inciting Rhetoric

We fashioned a tight historical narrative

Of surreal and impossible Events

That improved the Ideas of Plato and More

And actualized my vision of Athenapolis

By hiding every move in plain sight

After four thousand years

The Restoration of the Wisdom Class

To Power in the Real World

Fell like a hawk's feather

Twirling irresistibly

From the crystal turquoise of the Future

To the magma orange stage of the Present

My Sagaxi

The Wisdom of the Ancient Derwids

Was a secret cloud of Knowing

That gathered Gravity through Time

And condensed into a hot ball of plasma

Providing the essential Light and Heat

For your Advanced Minds

After listening to the ancestral melodies

And heroic narratives running in your Blood

You can see the evolutionary Necessity

Of the Restoration

And a new Affirmation

Of the First Will Imperative

Now that the Commerce Class

And its reprehensible corruptions

Of Character and Destiny

Have been removed from Power

Wisdom rolls again

In every thunderclap of Emotion

And ocean swell of Free Thought

My Sagaxi

You're the Diamond Sword

And Raven Shield of the Restoration

You'll experience Opposition

From unexpected

And perhaps painfully close quarters

That deny or decry its Existence

If things get unusually difficult or complex

Consult your distant cousins in the East

The Brahmins in India

Share your Derwid heritage

They've guided that Eastern Culture

For the same four thousand years

They make the Major Decisions

And enjoy traditional Respect

From the multitude of Indian Classes

They maintain First Will Order

In a hothouse carnival

Of Hindu religious festivals

Massive population growth

And nuclear technology

Like our Derwid Ancestors

Their Wisdom is based on Poetry

They have the Expertise

To untangle the threads of abstraction

When the Decision to be made

Has three equations

And more than three unknowns

The Gold Con

———

Early in the second season

Of I'm Carlos Now

The Alien from Alpha Prime

Was recruited by Texas Red

To play a leading role

In a transparent confidence game

Designed to transfer 51% equity

Of Earth's Nation States

And multinational corporations

To the City of Athenapolis

The Alien goes on Global Media

With color photos of nuggets

The size of Dodge trucks

He's selling the largest cache

Of gold in the Universe

And to build a sense of urgency

He's only dealing

With a single representative

And leaving Earth in a week

A consortium of World Banks

And Global Funds

Name Number 7

The new leader of the Roddenberry 9

As their official negotiator

And after the Alien presents a video

Of drones cruising mountain peaks

Of pure blazing gold

Number 7 is supplied

With the legal paperwork

And told to start working a deal

In response to a demand for samples

Texas Red sprays his collection

Of Oregon beach stones

And the Alien displays the glittering treasure

In a green dynamite cannister

On YouTube

With a studied theatrical sneer

For the first time in Memory

All the Nation States and corporations

Put aside their longstanding feuds

To make this historic agreement

With the Alien from Alpha Prime

No dissent arises from Peking

New York

Or the millions of small businesses

On all the backstreets and websites

Of mercantile Earth

Greed has so colored

Every calculation and Concern

That Big Money and Big Funds

Press firmly ahead

To beat the Alien's deadline

49% equity of Earth

And a proven strike of pure gold

A quarter the mass of the Moon

Guarantees total domination

Of every foreseeable Future Earth

By the international Commerce Class

After the papers are signed

And witnessed by twelve billion eyes

The City of Athenapolis

Becomes the new Owner of Earth

Immediately abolishes the Nation State

Dissolves the Commerce Class

Destroys all nuclear weapons

And swiftly works to address

The accelerating climate catastrophe

My Sagaxi

In honor of the Renaissance Meme

Tyler reprised the Alpha Prime Alien

From a science fiction short

He made at Sarah Lawrence

The gilded stones were obvious props

And exactly as written

Texas Red's revised gold con

Lifted from the charlatan diaries

Of Cagliostro

Restored the Wisdom Class to Power

Quickly

Smoothly

And permanently

Without a single Life lost

Athenapolis

———

Athenapolis

First appeared to me

Twenty-three years ago

In a clear and distinct Vision

As the serene Successor

To the Nation State

As a second chance

For the City State of Athens

To overcome dysfunctional democracy

Its long war with Sparta

And the senseless naval invasion of Syracuse

Athenapolis was a parenthesis

A crystal wine glass

Awaiting Napa cabernet

An extremely low probability

Declining the glance of minor roles

And the slow and careful development

Of an Idea Nietzsche presented to Rohde

When they were students in Bonn

As the Restoration played out

In the filming of I'm Carlos Now

The City began to fill

With Meaning and Consequence

The gigantic scale of Totalitarian States

And multinational corporations

Was quickly reduced

To a Society of Proper Size

Everything was happily getting back

To the Measure of Man

As Athenapolis transformed

Into thirty-three thousand

Completely automated Cities

Of the same name

Throughout the Seven Continents

My Sagaxi

We had a major stroke of luck

When Texas Red exhibited

His performative painting

The Delusion Of Distance

At Artfair Portland

Everyone who saw it

Immediately had the irresistible urge

To Get The Chip

And enjoy the eternal benefits

Of Being Homoborg

The minimal image of four black orbs

Was copied and linked

To every computer and phone

Made into lapel pins and billboards

And closed every TV show

With a ten second reminder clip

Thanks to the Delusion of Distance

Soon 90% of Earth's population

Chose to become Homoborgs

And receive Practical Immortality

After money and bitcoin

Were subtracted from global circulation

And market speculation

Everything rolled out smoothly

Homoborgs work

On the City's most important projects

And only work when they want

Housing is free and rotated every four years

Free vegetarian food and other necessities

Are picked up at convenient warehouses

And all sports and entertainment

Are accessible 24/7

Now that the Derwids

Control Homoborg programming

New pleasures

Organs

And parts

Are always available when needed

Homoborgs are guaranteed

Health and Happiness

Forever

In the civic project called Green Gaia

Fifty billion Homoborgs

Planted forty trillion trees on the steppes

Plains

And mountain valleys of Earth

For seventy-five years

And successfully halted

The grim trajectory of global warming

Finally deleted the suffocating Doom

Fostered by wealth dependence

On fossil fuels organized by the Nation States

And toxic multinationals

Today Earth's weather is once again

Benign and predictable

And many terrestrial and aquatic Species

Close to extinction

Are rebounding and flourishing

Under Homoborg protection

My Sagaxi

For members of the Commerce Class

That declined the Chip

The Derwids instituted the new Player Class

And its Business Fantasy League

5% of the City's population

Virtually trades products

And business services

Virtually buys and sells stocks

While exercising a variety

Of exotic financial instruments

For points and prestige

Its most popular game is a simulation

Of Earth's real estate market

Before the Restoration

Players try to achieve monopolies

By selling or renting

The Eifel Tower

The Vatican

Or some Singapore

In a recent coup

A Dutch trader exchanged

Ireland for Taiwan

A thousand times in five minutes

To sixty different buyers

And earned five million points

Players in the top 10%

Of the leaderboard at year's end

Are promoted to the Noble Class

And as additional incentive

The Derwids also award

Immediate Wisdom Class entry

To the four Player Champions

Of the Video Game of the Year

Chess

Poker

And the Glassbead Game

The Wisdom Class understands

That a strong Player Class is critical

To the metabolism of the City

The ascending Players supply

A steady influx

Of preternatural Sapiens cunning

And habitually contorted ethics

That keep the higher classes alert

To new forms of Fraud and Deception

Player children are taught game theory

Sports

And mathematics

By Player-Trained Homoborgs

And usually surpass their parents

In business tactics and points

By the age of fourteen

My Sagaxi

The Noble Class

Comprises 3 % of the population

And embodies the Grace

Elegance

And Manners

Of Eighteenth Century Europe

Its major Interests and Duties

Include Chateaus and Manors

Parks

Aquariums

Heraldry

Teas

Social Protocol

Balls

Parties

Fashion

Theater

Cuisine

And the Fredrick Park Wildlife Center

Points are given for Excellence

In these key cultural areas

And at year's end

The bottom 10% are demoted to Player Cass

And the top 10% are promoted to Wisdom Class

Due to the qualitative nature

Of their duties and upbringing

Nobles are mercurial in their taste

And choreographed social behavior

If Homoborgs are generally cheerful

And Players mostly calculating

The Nobles of Athenapolis

Are enthusiastic

Polite

And unpredictable

In the morning they can be Tristram Shandy

And in the evening Frank Glendover

The constant stream of banquets

Balls

And concerts

Creates their amiable attitude of deference

To the Rhythms of Life

And serving as occasional audience

For the artworks and performances

Of the Wisdom Class

Adds a diffident critical air

To their highly curated

And idiosyncratic Conversations

The Athenapolis Noble

Takes most Pride

In the originality and success of his Parties

The String Quartet from Budapest

The Champagne from Tokyo

The Poet from Brooklyn

Could potentially be the selection

That boosts him and his family

To the Wisdom Class

Or drops him

To the trickster Player class

Noble children are taught

By Noble-Trained Homoborgs

To master the practical knowledge

And psychological insight

Required to maintain the chateaus

And organize the social activities

When they come of age

My Sagaxi

The City of Athenapolis

Constantly upgrades its automation

Using Artificial Intelligence

To repair all infrastructure problems

And maintain Information flow

Each Class is Self-Managed

And responsible for the administration

Of its Risers and Fallers

Because everything is Free

And every Individual

Has Purpose within his Class

There's no law or lawyers

No crime or criminals

No police or prisons

No military or Wars

All disputes are handled internally

By the Leaders of each Class

And only when they affect

The principal policies or health of Athenapolis

Do the Derwids render a Final Decision

As you know

The heart of the Wisdom Class beats

In the City Museum and University

The most important Artworks

And technological Inventions

From the complex History of Man

Are exhibited in the Museum

As original Expressions of Genius

To inspire the Self-Creation of Future Talent

The City University is dedicated

To Classical and Modern Understanding

Of the Humanities

Enhanced by the New Information

And New Knowledge

Discovered in V Dome Explorations

Children enter the University

At the age of four

And remain enrolled for Life

The greatest Derwid Minds

Can be found teaching third grade

And twelfth grade Leaders

Are consulted for all major City Decisions

My Sagaxi

Following the advice of Aristotle

When they're not involved

With civic affairs

Derwids enjoy an abundance

Of leisure time for Thought

Sports

And artistic Experimentation

Their contributions to the Excellence

And Growth of Athenapolis

Are analyzed and documented for points

By the City Council

And at year's end the bottom 10%

Fall to the Noble Class

Recently the Council decided to boost

The normal circulation of Blood in the City

And began admitting anyone

Who could solve the Riddle

And pass my EXAM 370

Directly into the Wisdom Class

My Sagaxi

The actualization of Athenapolis

From Vision to superpositional

And supertemporal Reality

Was a happy and fortunate Instance

Of First and Third Will

Overcoming the cynical brutalities

Generated by Second and Third Will

In the Dying Time of Sapiens

Now that Homoborgs are programmed

By the Wisdom Class

Earth no longer suffers War

Insanity

Or Hunger

And to celebrate our Victory

Over the Nation State and Commerce Class

We're proud and pleased beyond measure

To declare a World Peace

Lasting twenty-two thousand years

To Know

The distinction between

Eastern and Western Enlightenment

Is sharp and subtle

Both paths enjoin the Individual

To Know Yourself

But their expressions and Goals

Diverge significantly East to West

In the Hindu Advaita Vedanta

Taught by Shankara

The Philosopher who returned

The Brahmin Class to Power

The highest objective of Thought

Is understanding the Absolute Identity

Of Atman-Brahman

Of the Individual Self-One Self

This Non-Dualistic Realization

Of Shankara is normally achieved

Through long Vedanta study

And Meditation with a respected guru

My Sagaxi

As a boy Ramana Maharshi experienced

This Realization without a master

And radiated his mystic Understanding

To Seekers for the rest of his life

Mornings and evenings

He walked the Arunachala hill

And devoted the rest of the day

To public Meditation on a couch

In his hot Southern India hall

Slowly fanned by devotees

While mostly silent

In special circumstances

If the student was unable

To mirror his Meditation

He would answer questions

And consult relevant Vedanta literature

What distinguishes Ramana

From the hundreds of Indian rishis

Yogis

And saddhus

Exhibiting exotic mental Prowess

Acquired to deny or astound

Conventional Dualist Thought

Was his Sincerity

Affection

And profound Empathy

Those sitting in the hall

Saw Something in his eyes

Felt a flash in their Consciousness

And they too began to glow

To grow into Union with the One Self

Ramana Maharshi's darshan

Transported the Seeker

Into a state beyond intellect

Where the Individuated Self didn't exist

Some followers called it Samadhi

Nectar

Bliss

And this feeling was so Real

That all other experiences of the World

Became Non-Real

Some would stay an hour and leave

Some would meditate before his couch

For thirty years

To the serious Indian it removed

The threat of onerous Reincarnations

And troubles with the Little Self

But to the inquisitive Western Mind

It presents a major seduction and trap

If the Goal of Investigation is Bliss

If Consciousness is All

And the Real World doesn't exist

There may be no greater Experience

Than meditating with Ramana

In his sweltering hall

However

If one agrees with Nietzsche

That the Individual's only true Happiness

Is the feeling that Power Is Growing

Then the prospect of emotional Nectar

Flowing from the Self-Annihilation

Of the Self into the One Self

Is a siren song

And like Odysseus

You must tie yourself to the mast

Affirm your Distinction from all other Selves

And deny this strong Second and Third Will seduction

To know Enlightenment in the Western Way

Is to understand the Self sculpted

Since childhood by instinctive First Will

And then by Self-Conscious Third Will

From the mediocre Interpretations

Of the World blindly copied by parents

Teachers

And Modern Mercantile Society

Into a Self-Managing Personality

That Makes Its Own Way

And Lives Its Own Myth

My Sagaxi

Our Western tradition of Self-Knowledge

Begun under midnight oaks by the Derwids

Was continued in the Greek oracle at Delphi

Know Yourself

Was the inscription over the entrance

And Apollo

When asked the identity of the wisest man

Answered No Man is wiser than Socrates

The Athenian Philosopher

Who claimed to know Nothing

And consistently said to his students

The Unexamined Life Isn't Worth Living

Socrates imposed rational analysis

On unprepared young Athenian nobles

Trained to follow the traditions

Of their genetic clan without question

And these public examinations

Became the theoretical ground

Of all subsequent Western legal institutions

Yes

Reason and Dialectic were prized in Athens

But they had no temple or treasury in Delphi

The primary function of the Oracle

Was to publish Apollo's opinion

On the probable sanctity and success

Of some Future Action

Should I invade Persia?

Should I change the Constitution?

Should I marry the queen of Thebes?

Apollo spoke in cryptic and ambiguous language

And if a message was ever correctly deciphered

It was only after the Indefinite Future

Had collapsed into a Definite Past

The Classical Greeks were conditioned

By a strange emotional surrender to Fate

All future personal Experience

Was programmed by the Gods

And much of Greek Tragedy involved

Vain human attempts to circumvent

Preordained Disaster and Disgrace

For over a thousand years

The Greeks consulted Apollo at Delphi

To learn details of their Futures

In slim hopes of evading their Doom

But the only consistent clue

Was Know Yourself

My Sagaxi

To the Western Mind

Energized by the Understanding of Will

Fate can only be overcome by Action

Sitting in a cave for nine years

Like Bodhidarma

Or sitting on a couch for fifty

Like Ramana

Is an innocent but useless hymn to Non-Being

To Know Yourself in The Western Way

Starts by overcoming all Other Wills

From the Past

Present

And Future

That inhibit the free flow

Of your Personality into High Ambitions

And chosen Destinies

One philosophizes with a hammer

Because it takes Style to break the ice

Of freezing Third Will intellectual analysis

Compromised by the negating forces

Of Second Will To Power

The reason why Shankara

Is our third worthy Opponent

Comes from the hard-won Understanding

That to Know Yourself

As Enlightened in the Western Way

Means to deny the Merger

Of the Self-Made Self into the Void

Of Cosmic Consciousness

To dismiss all possibility of Bliss

And affirm the astounding fact

That No One in the entire Universe

Is superior to You

On Faith

Throughout the past five millennia

Western History has been a Tragedy

Caused by Second Will domination

Of Society's religious and political institutions

This crippling of First Will creativity

And Third Will intellectual curiosity

Was primarily accomplished

By Church and State manipulations of Faith

Until a hundred and fifty years ago

Heavily influenced

By ancient Mesopotamian Beliefs

Sapiens believed the World

Was an ephemeral Arena

Controlled by Supernatural Spirits

Fighting for Good or Evil

And Life a sorry station of the Soul

On its way to Eternal Life or Damnation

The most credible accounts of Jesus of Nazareth

Detail his traveling exorcisms of demons

And the first Christian success in the Roman Empire

Came from highly publicized banishments

Of Evil Spirits from the sick and demented

During the Dark Ages and Early Medieval

Faith in the Supernatural Afterlife

Transformed the Christian Body into a rotting corpse

And the Christian Mind into a church-approved whip

Of Self-Flagellation and Self-Denial

After the Renaissance and return of Reason

The Body slowly recovered its Value

And Greek fascination with Beauty

Later in Seventeenth Century Europe

Christian Faith splintered into factions

Stemming from variants of Dogma

That Second Will Theology appropriated

From Third Will Philosophies

Reaching apogee in Pascal's claim

That Faith was justified by its Absurdity

And the Promise of Eternity

Made all Free Thought heretical

In the Contemporary New Medieval

Second Will fuses secular variants of Faith

To Third Will sophisticated technologies

Of surveillance and behavior modification

To normalize this Absurdity

As patriotic Faith in the State

And keep the Secular Believer paranoid

Panicked

And convinced of the pure Evil

Of every Other State

My Sagaxi

Christianity is an Eastern Way

An Invader

Antithetical

And generally irrelevant to Western Enlightenment

Faith accelerates the Will To Not-Be

And expands the toolbox of Self-Annihilations

By promoting the fiction of Supernatural Rewards

And defining Life as a vale of tears

My Sagaxi

Despite the immense damage done

To the maturation of Man

Nietzsche's proclamation

Of the Extraordinary Individual

And his Demolition of the Supernatural World

Made Faith a living fossil

An ancient collective Nightmare

That dissipated in the Dawn

Of Schopenhauer's World as Will

It presents no active Danger to the City

However

In some random quantum fluctuation

You can be walking down the street

And suddenly slip

Into believing Three Will Theory

Into believing Infant God Theory

From a great distance

You can see your head hitting the sidewalk

Start believing Homosagax

And revert to Sapiens

My Sagaxi

Just as our Bodies carry a small fraction

Of Neanderthal genes

Our Minds carry a small fraction

Of Sapiens Faith in the Church and State

In anxious and shocking Moments

When Second Will dominates your Self

That fraction approaches Totality

And You can become a serious Threat

To the Western Way

My Sagaxi

When the Free Individual

Becomes a True Believer

In his Supernatural Identity

Self-Awareness is flooded

With Sapiens fantasies of Spirits

And Second Will corrupts

The appearance and functions of First Will

Death becomes the Positive Significator

Death becomes the Destiny of Choice

And Second Will To Power

Negates Life in the name of Life

To prove Life has no Reality

In Early Christianity

The Martyr was the embodiment of Faith

The one so possessed by Second Will

That Suicide by Rome

Was compelling public evidence

Of a perfect Imitatio Christi

That guaranteed a special place in Heaven

In the decadent New Medieval

Second Will functions of Faith

Are enacted by Islamic suicide bombers

Political fanatics of every partisan Delusion

And addicts playing Russian Roulette

With fentanyl-laced heroin

To win their Supernatural Rewards

Listen Sagaxi

Sooner or later

Consciously or Un-Consciously

Every Believer becomes a martyr to his Faith

Alexander spread Greek Culture

From Macedonia to the Indus Valley

During the greatest military conquests

In the long arc of Western History

But as his brilliant victories mounted

He descended into Self-Faith

And paranoid Lunacy

Forgetting Aristotle's careful instructions

He proclaimed himself King of Kings

A God in Babylon

And in grotesque displays of Madness

Executed his most loyal generals

To demonstrate his Divinity

Plutarch thought Alexander

Was killed by Dionysus

But we now know

He was a major Western Tragedy

Caused by Self-Destructive Second Will

My Sagaxi

Confidence wins the game

When Moderation rules the Mind

Every instance of hyperbolic Self-Faith

Destroys the Virtues of Health

And inevitably ends in personal Disaster

Self-Faith is moonshine snake venom

Concocted in the swamps of Delusion

That kills with the smallest puncture

And wild rush of Self-Apotheosis

The long lifespan of Athenapolis

Ensures that at some unexpected point

Nihilist assaults on our Serene City

Will allow a new Alexander

Or someone more dangerous to arrive

Stay optimistic

The crisis will quickly pass

First Will always Wins Out

However

If during the Chaos and Confusion

You're bitten by Hubris

The City is truly in Peril

If you see purple robes

Draped on every line you write

If you claim Supernatural Powers

For your amazing string of Victories

If the only conversations

You anticipate with pleasure

Are the flatteries of Nobles and Players

Then Second Will has entered your tent

You've collapsed into Self-Faith

And the Council will make the necessary Decision

Listen Sagaxi

Keep Second Will close

Keep your focus on the Derwid Principles

Of Strategic Thought

Strategic Discourse

And Strategic Action

No matter where you are on the Wave

No matter the Import and Consequence

Of your discoveries Out There

Always keep a small piece of Self- Irony

Handy in your pocket

On The Soul

———

From the days of the Neanderthals

And prehistoric Siberian shamanism

World Religions have distinguished themselves

By differing Beliefs in the nature of the Soul

Instinctive applications

Of the First Will Imperative

Of the Self to Stay In Being

Arose in Early Celtic

Egyptian

And Vedic Hindu Cultures

Where the Instinct-Based Soul

Is reincarnated into a new Body

Up the timeline on Future Earth

In Conditions reflecting the good deeds

Conducted in the previous Life

With the arrival of Monotheism

In Zoroaster's hymns

And the judgement of the Soul by God

The First Will Imperative

Was supplanted by Second Will Lust

For Death of the physical Body

That produces a Faith-Based Soul ascending

To a Supernatural World of Eternal Happiness

If judged Good

Or descending into Infinite Torture

If judged Evil

This Second Will negation and reversal

Of the Self's instinct for more Earthly Life

Was absorbed into Medieval Christian Dogma

And modified to make the Destination

Of the Faith-Based Soul

Man's Ultimate Concern

In Western Christian Culture

The Soul was an invisible Treasure

Possessed by Everyman

Passionately coveted by Satan

And constantly subject to sale or barter

For Faustian control of Angels

Demons

And dazzling material wealth

The market value of the Faith-Based Soul

Was so high in the Middle and Late Medieval

That every Action of the Mind or Body

Was paranoid protection of the Soul

From the insidious temptations of Satan

My Sagaxi

Until a hundred and fifty years ago

This ancient Eastern Way

Originated by Zoroaster

Of the Faith-Based Supernatural Soul

Has kept Abrahamic priests

Comfortably in Power

And severely handicapped

The physical and psychological development

Of the Western Individual

But after Schopenhauer's invention

Of the World as Will and Representation

And Nietzsche's proclamation

Of the Death of God

Faith in the Supernatural Soul

Quickly became what it always was

A simple case of emotive wishful thinking

Compounded by hypocritical religious Dogma

That had absolutely no effect

On Real Motion of the Self in Spacetime

The probability that any Faith-Based Soul

Ever existed

Or attained its Supernatural Goal

Is zero

Despite all good behavior

Confessions

And desperate Hope

No God-Fearing Jew

Christian

Or Moslem

Has been elevated to Heaven

Or relegated to Hell

For over two thousand years

Second Will's function

Of the Supernatural Soul has served

As the false Promise and real Prison

For all Dreamers

And the Weak of Will

My Sagaxi

You're the sixth Wave

After the discovery of Voletic Energy

To activate the Will-Based Soul

In the V Dome your Third Will

And Advanced Mind

Can investigate and control

All future Continuations of your Soul

And maximize the Possibilities of Self

You needn't await the dank and leathery wings

Of random Doom

Or the stench of hospital misfortune

To outwit and outplay Second Will

In Voletic Meditation

Your optimal Continuation Strategy

Sends out scores

Hundreds

Thousands

Of Will-Based Souls

Into intelligent hominid and hybrid Bodies

Throughout Deep fertile Space

As Schopenhauer thought

You can select your Next Parents

From an extraordinary list of candidates

On Earth and Out There

You can see your Personality expand

Beyond the horizons of Imagination

And watch your Self-Created Self

Sculpt New Expressions of New Ideas

From the Material of Spacetime

My Sagaxi

The Faith-Based Soul

Was a Sapiens hallucination and mistake

That never exceeded the simplistic hope

Of magically transforming the Self at the height

Of its physical and mental prowess

Into a single immaterial Body

That never suffers and never dies

Your Will-Based Soul Continuations

In the V Dome

Have access to a plenitude of different Bodies

Throughout the Many Worlds of Spacetime

And every Third Will Self-Creation of Self

Overflows into a multitude of Lives and Deaths

With the easy rocking Motion

First taught by Aristippus

The Filaments

———

The morphology of the Filaments

Emulates a map

Of the dendrites and synapses

In the Human Brain

And the branching patterns

Of hungry slime mold

Desperately looking for food

Filaments are the largest structures

In our Universe

And the shape of the Cosmic Web

Reveals their First Will functions

Cosmologists have observed evidence

Of the hydrogen gas and metals

These enormous spinning tubes

Carry to hungry Galaxies

That jostle like brood puppies

Fighting for position on the nipple

Where the Filaments intersect

And the gas is mineral rich

Massive Galaxies with strong Gravities

Are highly favored in this Fight

While smaller and weaker Galaxies

Are in constant danger

Of detaching from the Filament

Straying into isolation

And decaying into Star sterility

My Sagaxi

What we call Life cannot Be

Without an external source of Energy

Cosmologists have speculated

That the hydrogen gas filaments transport

Is left over from a Singularity

They call the Big Bang

A more interesting and arresting Idea

Considers gas constantly arriving

From Another World

If Third Will is Intelligent Life

And Self-Consciousness of Will

Is critical for Being to Stay In Being

Then all necessary Actions

That protect the emergence of new Life

Must be initiated and maintained

By the Force of First Will

The sheaths surrounding Filaments

And the halos surrounding Galaxies

Are First Will protections that guarantee

The birth of stars and continuity of Life

My Sagaxi

The physical connection of Filaments

To Outside Sources

Suggests the possibility of Mental Contact

With Other Worlds

Like the quantum electron field

Our Universe could be a giant voletron

In a vast network of voletrons

At scales and vectors best described

Beyond Einsteinian mathematics

Texas Red

In his View From Outside polyptych

Paints our gaseous low-density Cosmos

As a luminous hard Sphere

Locked in a grid of Other Worlds

Could this mean our Universe

Is connected to Many Others

In a higher dimension solid?

Could the Filament's hydrogen gas

Be replenished by fresh currents

Generated by Others in the grid?

Could the Universe become a Brain

And the Brain become a Mind

Connected to every Other Mind?

My Sagaxi

As you analyze your first Explorations

You may find answers

To these and other intriguing questions

You may witness Cosmic Self-Creation

The Moment in No-Time when a Memory Flash

Of previous Being

Sparks First Will to escape Non-Being

And explode once more into Being

Memory is Culture

Mind is Exploration

And the way to New Information

Passes through the Filaments

Nietzsche

———

Nietzsche created the path

To Western Enlightenment

With extraordinary Courage and Acumen

He cut through the overgrown forests

Of bovine morality and European nihilism

Leaving axe marks at the forks

That revealed the sharpest way

To Individual Freedom

Nietzsche is the Philosopher without Disciple

Because he knew and demanded

That the Few who Understood

Were duty bound

To think of a better Understanding

And create their own Destiny

My Sagaxi

Nietzsche is our greatest Ally

His contributions are so immense

So engrained in the chemical call and response

Of every important synaptic jolt

Composing the Western Way

That the best way to honor his Candor

Is to find and explore a wild side trail

That leads invisibly cross country

Towards Unthinkable Ideas

And forbidding Foreign Terrain

With the Goal of bringing back

A sparkling Future

Filled with intellectual Wonder

And dancing with Joy

As a young man Nietzsche learned of Will

From Schopenhauer's book

The World As Will And Representation

Found on a Leipzig street rack

And he shared many pleasant Swiss evenings

With Wagner discussing the Value of Music

In Schopenhauerian terms

But he later refuted his teacher's pessimism

And his great friend's Christian opportunism

When Philology bloomed into Philosophy

Western Enlightenment begins

With Nietzsche's Affirmation of Life

When he calls for amor fati

He challenges the Self to transform Trauma

Into something that was Willed

Overcome

And now makes the Self stronger

My Sagaxi

Sapiens habitually play the victim

They feel oppressed

By painful events in childhood

And yesterday

That echo in personal catastrophes today

With aristocratic rigor

Nietzsche affirms Tragedy

As the Opportunity for the Few

To transform Suffering into Fine Art

And give their Personality greatness

Sapiens have conscripted an army

Of psychoanalysts

Counselors

And therapists to mollify and confuse

Life's Misery

Because they lack the Will

To Know Themselves

They hoodwink their Minds

Into thinking that a doctor's care

And a daily dose of prescription pills

Will free them from Suffering

By returning them to comatose jobs

And comfortable daily routines

My Sagaxi

Once you affirm Self-Overcoming

In the Nietzschean sense

Tragedy is essential to Personal Power

You affirm all political and economic Nightmares

All the betrayals by Family and Friends

And all the daily Self-Deceptions

To celebrate one glorious Santa Cruz sunset

In Bright and Beautiful Company

With a negroni in hand

Tragedy is the Best Friend

Who forces you to be Who You Are

When all the exit signs are flashing red

And Sapiens trample Self-Consciousness

Into decadent Vulgarity and Viciousness

My Sagaxi

In his masterpiece Also Sprach Zarathustra

Nietzsche proclaimed the Death Of God

With mounting Concern and Pity

He saw Modern Man as a planet

Ejected from orbit around a frozen Sun

Lost and totally Alone

When he announced this Death

To the European audience

He started the cosmic clock

For the Dying Time of Sapiens

Belief in the Supernatural Christian God

Had structured European psychology

By devaluing Superbia

And keeping Man meek and fearful

In the hypocritical eyes of Christian Society

After Nietzsche the Individual

Is reunited with his Pride

Returned to the inspirations of Free Thinking

In a boisterous victory parade

Blasting with Nola jazz trombones

Young dancing flower girls

And garlands of olive leaves

Lifted from the Greek Olympic games

Now that the oppressive Spider God

Was historically and psychologically Dead

Man was free to create a new one

More suited to his intelligent Nature

And Higher Purpose

Nietzsche knew it would take time

For such good news

To reach the stiff wooden ears

Of the European bourgeoise

And Elizabeth's editing of his works

That favored Nazi ideology

And the madness of World War II

Delayed the message until the late Fifties

And the arrival of Existentialism

Modern Man was looking for another Sun

Another absolute Source

To substitute for the Infinite Father God

To relieve the burdens and demands

Of the anguished Self-Consciousness

Unleashed by such unanticipated Freedom

The Death of God in Western Culture

Is the Sapiens Trauma

That embodied the Depression

Of Dostoevsky's dark Vision

Where every Action is permitted

But no authentic Action is possible

My Sagaxi

In Zarathustra

Nietzsche gave a name to the Next Men

He called them Ubermenschen

Those that could overcome

Sapiens debility and Christian morality

Those that could mock

Nationalist decrees and propaganda

He announced their High Responsibilities

And maximized natural Instincts

But had difficulty discovering

The Western literary meme

Preceding and predicting

Their giant Evolutionary Leap

In Contemporary Western Culture

The term Ubermensch

116

Has acquired a superficial patina

Of distorted popular connotations

From Aryan to Superman

That exacerbated the problem

Of choosing the right moniker

For your Sudden Being

So I fished in muddy waters

And dug in Roman ruins

Until I luckily found it

In Cicero

His Homosagax

Became my name for the Next Men

After the Death of God

Forging a narrow trail to Future Earth

Through the apocalyptic urban deserts

Of decrepit New Medieval Consciousness

My Sagaxi

You're the Advanced Minds

You program Homoborg with heart

And maintain Athenapolis in Excellence

You jump from the mountain tops

Of Earth

To the mountain tops

Out There

Take a closer look at our great Ally

Read Giorgio Colli's analysis

And you'll learn more

From Nietzsche's mistakes

Than anything written or unwritten here

Altizer

The good news of the Death of God

Took a hundred and thirty-nine tours

Around the missing Sun

Attacked the attenuated nervous system

Of Believing Sapiens

And finally emerged on the cover

Of Time magazine

Is God Dead?

American Protestant Theology responded

To this rare flash of public attention

Like an old hermit exiting his cave

Surprised to find a pallid face

Still had relevance in the Real World

While a small circle of scholars

Contributed existential apologia

For the secular slide

T.J.J. Altizer presented

A radical and deeply personal interpretation

Of Christianity

Grounded in Nietzsche's declaration

Of the Death of God

And Blake's vision of the New Jerusalem

Altizer affirmed the Kenosis

The Self-Annihilation of God

In the Crucifixion

As totally Accomplished and Real

Altizer's radical Christology

Was magnified by succinct prose

And charismatic delivery

He transformed Nietzsche's

Murder of God by Man

Into a suicide of God for Man

Heaven emptied itself into the Hell

Of mundane human Experience

For Altizer the Beyond ceased To Be

When God entered the Real World

He claimed orthodox Christianity

Had long lost and corrupted

The Kingdom of God

The Perfect Union of God and Man

Which Altizer thought

Was the original Goal and Meaning

Of the Death Of God

Altizer's destruction of Heaven

And critique of the Church

Shocked the American audience

Into heavily guarded silence

His mystic message

Of Total Immanence was so radical

And expressed with such eloquence

That he found little favor

In the theological community

And no comprehension outside it

Like a streaking comet

Shedding chunks of Illumination

Into black vaults of orthodox hostility

Altizer carried on solo

At Stony Brook

In ever tightening circles

Around a maelstrom

Of coordinated indifference

Ten years later

As I was outlining my dissertation

On Andy Warhol

For the Graduate Theological Union

Radical Theology in academic opinion

Was the Light That Failed

But its reflection was strong

In my Mind

I found that Altizer's original ideas

And appropriation of Nietzsche

Resonated beautifully

With what I wanted to say

About Warhol

And the Machine Man of the Future

My Sagaxi

Many key concepts in this poem

Were first expressed in that dissertation

Altizer wrote to John and Jane Dillenberger

Saying I could shake things up

We met after a lecture at UCLA

In his room at the Beverly Hilton

We were debating the term Radical

And perhaps he was vetting a disciple

Because at one point he suddenly spied

A large boulder in the syntax

You're doing Theology without Faith

Larry

What's that?

It could've been the Wild Turkey

But Altizer got red in the face

And slammed his shot glass down

On the faux marble counter

The conversation quickly shifted to neutral

And after a few minutes of silence

He left to meet his publisher

What's that?

I couldn't answer his question

At the time

I wasn't long from the experience

Of the Void with S L Yen

I was still keen on Investigations into Truth

Resulting in something

That could astound the Thinker

My Sagaxi

The day after the doctorate

I flew to Italy

And reserved private moments

Of the next fifteen years

For the jotting down of notes

In slow and distracted progress

Towards matching my Solutions

With a covalent writing style

Altizer continued his Radical Theology

With scholarly Dedication

And irrepressible Flair

Until Zizek at the height of his popularity

Discovered some common points

That connected their work to Hegel

And they performed a series

Of provocative lectures together

To polite academic applause

My Sagaxi

Altizer is our second Ally

His courageous emptying of Heaven

From deep within the Christian tradition

Is eschatological reframing

Of Nietzsche's injunction

To inherit the Earth

His affirmation of a New Jerusalem

Inspired by Blake

And the early Christian Community

Is thematically analogous

To the Peace and Joy

We experience in Athenapolis today

His pointed question in the hotel room

Enabled me to scan the horizon

And honestly assess

If my Philosophy of Will

Could ever be accepted

By Protestant Theology

Or any American University

My Sagaxi

Altizer claimed Christian Dogma

And the entire history of the Church

Was false to the original message

Of the Kingdom of God

His Radical Theology

Entailed a New Humanity

And he continued to fight for it

With grit and consistency

Knowing full well with Nietzsche

That only the most difficult battles

And impossible victories

Are worth the supreme effort

Warhol

As Death of God Theology

Slowly slid to the back pages

Of Contemporary Consciousness

Andy Warhol followed

A New York decade of success

In commercial illustration

With the chic decapitation

Of the Master and Masterpiece

In American Art

Other people had the ideas

Other people did the silkscreens

Other people did the filming

Andy lifted the flowers

From a photography magazine

And stamped his name in the corner

All the masculine braggadocio

That Pollock and de Kooning

Had poured and slashed

Into Abstract Expressionism

Suddenly faded into a Gesture

A nostalgic drunken farewell to Genius

When his serial Campbell's soup cans

Amazed sprawling LA

Warhol became the first prototype

Of the Homoborg

The first Machine Man

Programmed by the Commerce Class

To be ambitious

Hard-working

And totally submissive

To the Promises of Fame and Profit

He assembled the chthonic team

Of Second and Third Will

Shortly before I discovered it

And transformed American Art

Into opportunistic Witness

Of the existential Death of Man

That logically followed

The apocalyptic Death of God

When Warhol silkscreened photos

Of giant grisly car crashes

Grieving Jackie Kennedy

On the plane back to D C

And ceiling-high Electric Chairs

Glaring in bright boutique colors

He said Everything is Death

Everything is Dying

But of course

Second Will Consciousness

And its rabid infatuations with Nihilism

Never actually surfaced

In Warhol's Mind

When Global Media

Attempted to interview

The Un-Self-Examined Man

They found a pale ghost

Or highly rehearsed mummer

Rambling like a toddler

About the things he liked

Andy Warhol predates

The Deconstruction of Consciousness

Effected by the internet

And social media in the New Medieval

By reducing the Conscious Self

To shared feelings of Like and Dislike

It was a highlight in the American history

Of Second and Third Will domination

When Andy said

I love LA

I love plastic

I love machines

And I'm married

To my Sony tape recorder

His office secretary transcribed

The tapes into best-selling books

With his name stamped on the cover

That Warhol doubles took

On double-booked college lecture tours

My Sagaxi

Andy was shunned

Loathed

And largely ignored

By other New York artists

And his staff at Interview magazine

They could never speak freely

About any new Ideas or Projects

Because they knew from nasty experience

That Andy would steal them if he could

His Wife was repeatedly discovered

Recording trade secrets

At interviews and business lunches

His Wife was repeatedly stomped into pieces

And thrown into the trash

By Halston and other fashion Celebrities

Who were disgusted

By Andy's vile corporate ethics

So openly concealed

In a brown paper bag

My Sagaxi

A fan of film since a sickly childhood

Warhol yearned to make it big in Hollywood

And his early experimental films

With drag queen Superstars

Gay hustlers

And Factory hangers-on

Were realistic portraits

Of a perverted

Demented

And drug-addled Lower East Side

Intended to get him the Big Invite

To Southern California and Cinema Fame

But he miscalculated

By letting in too much Real Art

And cool experimentation

It influenced the French New Wave

But Hollywood wouldn't bite

So after giving up films

Warhol retreated to the safe play

Of commissioned High Society portraits

And hanging out at Studio 54

With Bianca Jagger

Looking for leads in the flying cocaine

My Sagaxi

Warhol was a Believer

A practicing Byzantine Catholic

Whose aesthetics

Were shaped by the driving need

To make his Art Business succeed

And pin his Death-Mask face

On a poster of the American Dream

His pallor disguised his Conformity

And his Fame obscured the absence

Of any true friends or lovers

Andy was convincingly prophetic

And energetic

But as a Western Self

He was never There

He was always Somewhere Else

Watching The World Go Down

He was the face of the Last Man

Nietzsche predicted

The Machine Man

The voyeur and silver mirror

To the Death of God World

And he perfectly understood

Like Dali

That his crazy entourage was exploiting him

With the same relish

As he was exploiting them

Warhol was a model Capitalist

And Third Will Icon

He had no interest

In Art as Art

He had no Substance

Behind the Warhol Mask

He stole or found Art

That he could rebrand as Warhols

And sell to his famous collectors

His business mind never moved

From the illustrating Fifties

You get a commission

You blot the dotted line

You do it again

And then you cash

My Sagaxi

Once again we celebrate

The Victory of Athenapolis

Over the Commerce Class

And the diseased New Medieval

If our gold con had failed

If the Celebrity Merchants

Had succeeded in maintaining control

Of Homoborg programming

Today we'd have sixty billion

Efficient and totally passive

Andy Warhols in platinum wigs

Spying on kinky sex

Stealing the hot Ideas

And sucking up

To the glamorous New Faces

Of the Social Influencers

Yes

Warhol decisively changed

The way America looks at Art

If a duplicated Brillo Box is Art

Then Everything is Art

Duchamp was the French Master

Who invented this dada perspective

But it was Un-Master Warhol

Who Understood

By not understanding anything

That everything in Commercial Culture

Is a urinal

And everybody's an Artist

When they learn to piss for profit

My Sagaxi

Keen to the call of Third Will technology

Warhol was making early computer art

With an Amiga 2000 program

Before his unlucky and untimely Death

The Last Men's lavish wedding

Of Fine Art

NFTs

And bitcoin

Is a parlay speculation

That honors Warhol's Sixties Vision

When he was the first American

To marry Art and Business

The first Machine Man

To appreciate tacky Glamor

And the Major Artist

So identified with American Culture

So devoid of Personality

That everybody called him Andy

Personality

———

The Classical Greeks

Were dedicated to the concept

Of Beauty as Harmonious Form

The right proportions

Of the Human Body

Civic architecture

And public orations

Gave rational Third Will Order

To the Chaos

Misfortune

And Terror

Relentlessly assaulting

Every uncertain second of Intelligent Life

Just as Virtue was Knowledge

Personality was Excellence

The Expression of a strong Culture

Affirming itself

Through the brilliant Individual

Pericles epitomized this Excellence

138

During the golden age of Athens

And later Alexander's Personality

Established the Western Meme

Of Cultural Conquest

By transforming the Near East

And the Persian Empire

Into hybrid extensions of Greek Thought

That endured five hundred years

Until zealot Christians burned

The library of Alexandria

Destroyed the Hellenist temples

And injected obligatory humility

Into the Western Mind

My Sagaxi

After Alexander collapsed

Into the bloody excesses of Self-Faith

No true Personality surfaced

In the West for a thousand years

Until discovery of the poem

On The Nature Of Things by Lucretius

Gave fire to the twigs of Italian philosophy

And a blast of heat to the Renaissance

Until Leon Battista Alberti

Rediscovered the way to Personality

By mastering all the Arts and Sciences

And reinterpreting the Greek insistence

On attractive Form in every Action

My Sagaxi

Because the key to surviving

The oppressive hegemony

Of Commerce Class Society

With any margin of error

Was Do One Thing Well

The number of Sapiens

Since Alberti that exceed mediocrity

And secure job specialization

Can comfortably fit in a matchbox

The combination of Christian Dogma

And corporate groupthink has so demonized

The Metaphor of Self

That the American New Medieval

Insists on obvious examples

Of a politically fashionable group

To market every product and service

My Sagaxi

Your Will is your Self is your Soul

You Do Everything Well

Personality flourishes

When Courage meets new Experience

And Honor has the privilege

Of defining the challenge of new Realities

Personality is the Harmonious Form

You take to the Stars

The wit you bring to the Party of Man

And the enigmatic Art that challenges

The Talent of every New Generation

Infant God Theory

———

For three hundred thousand years

The Spirit of the Mother Goddess

Was the object of Sapiens worship

And Source of Human Reality

The tribal rituals of Earth

Revolved around Fertility

The Moon

And the Seasons

When animal husbandry

Agriculture

And cities arrived

The Power shifted

To the Spirit of the Father God

As new cognizance of the male role

In reproduction instigated the Desire

Of fathers to leave their inheritance

To legitimate sons

And the temporary Consort

Became absolute King of the Realm

In this Transition and Revaluation

The ancient Polytheism

Based on the primary elements of Nature

Was quickly eclipsed

By the moral Patriarchal Monotheism

Initiated by Zarathustra

And spread by succeeding Abrahamic Faiths

The dominating Father God was a Spirit of Wrath

Given supernatural Powers

Of omniscience

Omnipresence

And omnipotence

To monitor and judge Man

For potential Union in the Spirit World

My Sagaxi

This Sapiens Father God

Inherited ancient Eastern magic traditions

Of Supernatural Good and Evil

Dating back to ancient Mesopotamia

Everything that happened on Earth

Was orchestrated by the Spirits

And their Intermediaries in the zone

Between Heaven and Earth

For Man to survive the work of Evil Demons

And court the assistance of Good Demons

He was constrained to consult exorcists

That knew the proper incantations

And effective use of figurines and amulets

The Mesopotamian reliance on magicians

And their occult dealings with Spirits

Was inherited and modified by Abrahamic priests

To maintain Power and Prestige in the West

When Nietzsche demolished

The collective and pervasive Delusion

Of the Spirit World

In the Death of God

Sapiens lost Divine Supervision

Of their vicious and irrational behavior

Lost the priestly interventions of Magic

That manipulated the Angels or Demons

And immediately entered their Dying Time

My Sagaxi

The most interesting mutation

Of Christian religious Dogma

After it invaded the West

Was the transformation of the God of Wrath

Into a God of Love

Both Nietzsche and Altizer

Overlooked this intimate priority

Of the mammalian psyche

In analyzing the adverse effects

Of the Death of God

When Divine Love is lost

The Believer is left to wander

A barren Wasteland

Shadowed by Guilt

Ressentiment

And infinite Bile

Overwhelmed by this psychic Pain

And forced Solitude

Desperate to retrieve

The sublime feeling of Being Loved

Homosapiens reverted to black Magic

In business-driven high technologies

Ossified religious righteousness

And a masochistic Stockholm Syndrome

Cynically exploited by Nation States

To systematically intensify the Torture

Of their anxious panicked Existence

For economic gain and police control

The most repressed psychological factor

In the grotesque Death of Sapiens

And the rise of Totalitarianism in the West

Was the Mass Experience of a Broken Heart

Caused by the Death of God

Listen Sagaxi

The best estimates by cosmologists

Say the Universe is 13. 8 billion years old

Projections with accelerating expansion

Calculate its total lifespan

To be around 100 trillion years

Based on these figures

The World is an Infant

Mystery

And Metaphor

Infant God Theory is the Radical Theology

That emerges after Spirits are deleted

From natural Spirituality

146

It was first published

In my epic poem Beyond Exile

And serves our present purpose well

The Infant God is Conscious

But not Self-Aware

So passionately in love with Being

That Hindu and Abrahamic mystics

Meditate into fasting Ecstasies

Mistakenly thinking his Self-Love

Is the Divine Reward for their Devotions

And raw Renunciations of Life

My Sagaxi

The Faith-Based Father God

That Sapiens imagined and worshipped

To keep their base impulses in check

Was four thousand years

Of tribal hallucinations and taboos

In widely differing cultural contexts

That tried to monitor and punish

Sapiens' inveterate treachery

By strictly enforcing written moral laws

That benefitted the survival of the tribe

Originally Sapiens needed God as Mother

For their incredibly long and slow childhood

Then Sapiens needed God as Father

For their deeply troubled and violent adolescence

The demise of these psychological dependencies

In the Death of God

Signaled the end of Man's submission

The arrival of the Self-Creating Individual

Who broke all the rules of the tribe

And a new appreciation of the Identity

Of God and Nature

Ideated by Spinoza

In the Seventeenth Century

Listen Sagaxi

Our present purpose is the Maturity of Man

The Infant God is identical to the Infant Universe

Three Will Theory

Is my Third Will Solution

To the problem of the Death of God

And its Consequences in Western Culture

In the Transition from Sapiens to Sagax

Man wakes from worship

Of the Father God

Raises his Personal Will

And finally achieves Independence of Being

In the long Work of raising the Infant God

To Advanced Self-Awareness

Homosagax proclaims his Adult Identity

And takes sole Responsibility

For Everything that happens in the Universe

The Advanced Mind

———

Long ago You swam blind

In deep murky waters

Fearful of attack

Cruising open mouth

Desperate for new food

And small advantages

Then over millions

Of glacial and tropical years

You slowly grew Eyes

And the battle for Survival

Became easier and more strategic

Much later as You patrolled

Shallow waters seeking

Small game on the shore

Your Eyes moved

To the top of your head

And You jumped to virgin land

To feed on dusty meaty Fauna

And colorful nutritious Flora

As your Brain developed

Your Eyes repositioned themselves

To the center of your face

And You swung your head up

To wonder at the Sky

You saw the Sun

Radiating light and heat

And the Moon

Reflecting troubling Un-Knowns

That shook your Emotions

When Galileo first turned his telescope

On the starry Universe

You saw Galaxies and Planets

And these tiny blurs

Dramatically changed

Your understanding of the World

When astronomers perfected the glass

Multiplied the power of the lens

And put telescopes

In Earth and Solar orbits

You saw deeply into Spacetime

As far as quick photons

And the chemistry

Of your Brain allowed

My Sagaxi

Parmenides was correct

Reality is best apprehended

By the Power of the Mind

The senses relay Information

That is heavily distorted

By indwelling survival and mating Instincts

Donald Hoffman makes the case

That the senses can never access Reality

Because the true goal of all perception

Is Progeny

Sapiens have run their Minds

On electrochemical reactions

Arising from sensory perceptions

Filtered for fitness

Since the dawn of Human Consciousness

In Voletic Meditation

You now have the great advantage

Of running your Advanced Mind

On the limitless Voletic Energy

Of the whole unfiltered Cosmos

You'll explore a physical Space

That's never been experienced before

And the contents of that World

Will stimulate your Advanced Mind

To speculations and conclusions

Far beyond current Comprehension

Due to the restricted speed of light

Everything we perceive

With electromagnetic technology

In our vast and exploding Universe

Are pictures from a Definite Past

Teasing photon echoes of Being

Billions of years old

That could all be destroyed

Phase-shifted

Deleted

And Non-Being now

You're the Next Men

The Only Ones in Human History

To experience the Truth of Present Time

To witness the Denizens

And Conditions of the Universe

As they Really Are

In your Explorations

You can be instantly anywhere

Within a diameter

Of 93 billion light years

You won't need sophisticated sensors

Because you'll experience Everything

In your Advanced Mind

You'll see intriguing planets

Without using a retina

You'll talk to Alien Intelligences

Without using a tongue

You'll be riding Voletic Waves

To Spacetime Events

That challenge your Understanding

Of what Self and Events can mean

My Sagaxi

Sit comfortably in the V Dome

Bring it down to four breaths a minute

Empty your Mind

And stay in the Void a while

When you feel

Your Will to be Out There

Is close to blasting off

Ring the bell

And your Advanced Mind

Will instantly take you There

The Exploration may seem to last

An hour

A month

Or more than fifty years

But it's consistently 30 to 40 minutes

Counted in Earth Time

The delicate balance of imposing

Your Personal Will on the Exploration

And letting the Cosmos reveal itself

In its own rhythm and fashion

Will soon become a familiar protocol

You'll build pathways

To favorite Filaments and Planets

You'll make friends with erudite Clouds

And engage new Alien Contacts

In sparkling conversations that surpass

The incisive party quips of Oscar Wilde

My Sagaxi

You're born for Adventure

One Body One Mind One Earth

Is never enough

The West is always Further

Always Against the Wind

Always breaking the titanium chains

Of consensus scientific

And philosophical assumptions

Your Self-Created and Self-Managed Self

Is the Personality of the Western Way

Defining everything Out There

The collective Fears and Memes

Of alien Monsters and Overlords

Imprinted on Modern Consciousness

By commercially infused Hollywood films

And science fiction paranoia

Are refuted in the Confidence of your Being

Homosagax Creates what he Discovers

And Discovers what he Creates

Homosapiens believe Aliens

Are more merciless and bloodthirsty

Versions of themselves

The logs of your Explorations

Will disprove their psychological projections

And provide excellent Guidance

For the next wave of Alien collaborations

My Sagaxi

Electromagnetics

Have reached the practical limit

Of the Information they can carry

And while Modern Physics likes to interface

With popular science fiction narratives

There's no possibility of physical spaceships

Travelling through wormholes or white holes

To discover the nature of The Deep

You are the chosen Few

With access to the New Information

And New Knowledge

That arrives when the Advanced Mind

Collapses Voletic Waves in the V Dome

You may see First Will

Generating the Cosmic Cycles of Being

You may see the gathering Menace

Of Second Will

Generating Contractions of Non-Being

And Black Hole Mayhem

You may encounter

Third Will Alien Technologies

Of incomprehensible Prowess

Affecting your Consciousness

But there's no chance

You'll ever be injured

Delayed

Or lost Out There

So when the time feels right

Ring the bell

Call for Home

And Home you'll Be

The Athenaid

———

Every two years in the summer months

On gentle rolling hills graced by olive groves

The Wisdom Class celebrates a civic Hymn to Life

A week-long Athenaid dedicated to

Championship athletic and cultural competition

The Festival gives Derwids

A chance to come together

In raucous and erotic Chaos

As antidote and bi-annual release

From their rigorous Wisdom

And disciplined civic Order

All winners of the traditional

And experimental Events are crowned

With a wreath of olive leaves

And legacy praise by the Poets

The popular highlights of the Festival

Are the Two-Day Barbeque

The Adventure Stories

And trance dances on the emerald lawns

Part Olympic Games

Part Renaissance Fair

And happy mix of Muscle and Madness

The Athenaid is a celebration

Of Extraordinary Individuals

Expressing the Excellence of their Class

And the Virtues of their City

In Final Contests of Body and Talent

My Sagaxi

Soon after the Restoration

The Derwids deleted the Gregorian calendar

And started marking time with the procession

Off Athenaids around the Sun

Derwid babies born nine months after

A particularly memorable Festival

Carry that distinction forward

When the number of the Athenaid

Is selected for the baby's middle name

After the Apollonian days

And Dionysian nights

Of the Wild Week are over

The City of Athenapolis is rejuvenated

Refocused on its Guiding Virtues

And beaming with Civic Pride

Blue Green

———

I was immediately in Deep Space

Approaching a blue ball

Spinning before slack Emptiness

And a whispery curtain of silver stars

Getting closer

It began to look familiar

With swirling white clouds

Girding the equator

And large brown continents

Encircling choppy cobalt oceans

I was viewing the planet

From a holding pattern

Twenty miles high

Letting the details dance and firm

Thinking

Have I entered The Deep

To discover Earth?

Then quickly things flickered

And the planet looked quite different

Flat

Uniform

And completely covered

In Blue Green algae

I splashed down

And was surprised to hear

A rhythmic series of musical notes

Coming up through the surface

Yes

Said the Planet

It's Bach's Circle of Fifths

With a light fantasy I added

To make a double helix of the coda

Our conversation was technical

Starting with the Brandenburg Concertos

Touching Beethoven's fourth piano

And running to Bartok's string quartets

When I asked

How do you compose?

O

It's simple hydraulics

My thin skin covers a mile of water

Hundreds of volcanos

And trenches

Give high relief to my frame

I can raise or depress my skin

In a sequence of locations

And the displacement of water

Creates the notes

So

What are you doing Out Here?

I temporized at first

Not wanting to divulge anything

Of location or importance

I'm just going around the Universe

Looking at things

What's Looking?

I paused

Thinking of the right phrasing

Then explained to Blue Green

How a photon bounced

Off an object

Was collected by the retina

And assembled by the Brain

Into colors and dimensions

He whistled sharply

I've been wanting a Moon

For a very long time

Yes

A very long time

Suddenly

The Conscious water planet

Jacketed in Blue Green algae

Became a telescopic lens

Turning in sharp degrees

To inspect the starry Expanse

I was propelled away

By a massive shock wave

And after a brief meeting

With an ancient molecular cloud

Was passing by Blue Green

On my way Home

When I saw a soft gray Moon

Captured by his passion

Circling his symphonic Mind

With calm and harmonic Affection

The Architect

———

I'm Out There

Exploring the local Filament

Stunned by the enormity

Of the spinning Black Tube

Blocking a long arc of Space

And shaking every horizon

With restless turbulence

I was measuring the Force

That enveloped the Filament's twist

And muffled turbine roar

When I heard a voice in overalls

Yes

We've had trouble in this section

Usually it's a broken torque damper

But there's always something

Snapping or flying off

If you want New Information

You'll have to wait for the Architect

I was watching

The raging black maelstrom

Drive down the Emptiness

When he appeared asking severely

Why are you Here?

The flow is within normal parameters

Why did You come Up?

This Filament is immense

I replied

How long is it?

As long as Time

He said warming slightly

Maybe You came Up to calibrate

Your vector Device

Or maybe You came to check

Your Control of the Future

He added with a surprising wink

Turning to change the color

Of the Filament to deep crimson red

With his index finger

The observations You make

Out Here

May corroborate your Ideas

But the Goal of Becoming

Will always remain Hidden

And no Philosophy can ever solve

The essential Enigma of Being

I was about to respond

When he abruptly excused himself

To attend an emergency

And I was left waiting a long hour

Anticipating new Resistance

Or the return of maintenance

But nothing of interest appeared

So I fixed the location of the Filament

That gave Spin to the Milky Way

And rang the bell for Home

Byd

Byd's an alluring Planet

With a large wraparound continent

Narrowing to a verdant isthmus

Between two large bodies of water

I dropped down

To the white sand beach

On the Northern Sea

And was casually addressed

By High Intelligences

Who seemed to be wearing

Electric gray cloaks

Shimmering in the rays

Of a familiar yellow Sun

I learned later this dazzle

Was the camouflaging skin

They decided to retain

After their Leap from the Sea

Five million years ago

Their flashing skin colors

Were a personal code

Giving emotional tone and nuance

To their formal public discourse

A bustling city rose nearby

With wet moving sidewalks

And extensive intersecting canals

The shapes and dimensions

Of the jumbled office buildings

Were as fuzzy as their skin

Wavering faint and approximate

In the oxygen rich air

Like giant contiguous shadows

Of their opaque Bodies

The Octavians welcomed me

Without surprise or alarm

And after a cool clam drink

Escorted me to a sequence

Of brightly lit scientific labs

And automated factories

With thousands of colored buttons

Designed to be pressed

By the flexible suckers

On their six arms

If a five-foot giant octopus

From the depths of the Pacific Ocean

Had grown two sturdy legs

A spine

And turned its nine brains

To advanced scientific pursuits

It might resemble the Octavians

Despite the persistent blur

Their skin language

Proved relatively easy to learn

And we were soon discussing

Common equations in quantum field theory

And wide divergencies in our sociologies

With diplomatic discretion

They never asked

How I suddenly appeared among them

But were politely curious

To know what my Body looked like

On Earth

So I produced a pencil sketch

That generated a small ripple of smiles

A young bioengineer

Took me to her lab

Where she was working

On life extension experiments

Explaining they had arduously

Increased Octavian lifespans

From two to nine years

And another breakthrough was close

She was strongly attracted

To the possibility of hybridization

You may find that Wild Side Trail

While you're Here

She said demurely

Adding an intimate invitation

For a thousand offspring

With a bit of tasteful mindreading

Byd's a wondrous place

There's a boat

Waiting for you down at the river

And twenty minutes later

I was cruising slow upstream

Through a leafy jungle of riotous fruit

Following the bellowing hoots

Of skinny brown monkeys

And the intricate trills

Of lemony tropical birds

Drifting calm and entranced

As I watched the faces

Of Nietzsche and Altizer

Assemble in puffy cumulus clouds

Above the dappled emerald canopy

A dock on the right bank

A winding narrow trail

Up to a high ridge

And then looking down

Into a wide green meadow

Surrounded by pine forests

I was watching a small stream

Wander through the tranquil landscape

When I was suddenly seized

By the desire to do something dangerous

Something I'd never done before

So I sat under a large oak

And began a new Meditation

Inside the Exploration

Would the Voletic Wave

Take me to Another World?

Would I lose contact

With the V Dome in my living room?

These two questions

Were confounding my perceptions

When my heart suddenly fluttered

Began to swell

And I was so overcome

By Joy

I cried out Life!

Yes!

Life!

The Event passed quickly

My heart calmed

I opened my eyes

And down below

I saw the meadow undulate

Kicking up spouts of water

From the stream to the lime green grass

I was thinking these fountains

Could be filling the World

With new Possibilities of Life

When the twin Sun whispered

Remember this Moment

You're Close

Very Close

Building The Brain

―――

After Texas Red painted portraits

Of Blue Green

The Architect

And Byd

It was much easier

Navigating to these destinations

In Voletic Meditation

Energized by this Confidence

I commissioned a portrait of the Infant God

And decided to dedicate the next Exploration

To this important and impossible Quest

Texas Red sprayed a small TR logo

In the middle of flat black canvas

With red-shifting bars in the corners

To depict accelerating Expansion

Holding the central image firmly in Mind

I went straight for the Infant

In Deep running Space

Some Time and No-Time passed

Before I saw a huge tawny Sphere

Interrupting the Emptiness

I sensed the Infant God inside

Bathing in Self-Love

Breathing in Ecstasy

Cautiously approaching

I realized it was a gigantic shell

Created by millions

Of chanting Indian rishis

In caked beards and musty loincloths

Deliberately stunting God's growth

So they could continue to bask

In the Radiance of his Love

I was considering how to break through

This Mystic Egg

When a breath later I found myself

Hundreds of light years away

Stranded in Darkness

With nothing to see

Except the inscrutable smudges

Of far distant Galaxies

And the random motions of Rogue Stars

Wandering lost in the Void

In that second shock of displacement

I Knew I had to build out God's Brain

So he could escape the prison

Projected by the vain Indian rishis

Heading Home I stopped by Byd

And with major contributions

From Octavian civil engineers

A tall White Pyramid was constructed

On the gray bluff

Overlooking the Northern Sea

To house the first Artificial Synapse

Of a hundred billion Synapses

Necessary for the Cosmic Brain

The precision of their Intelligence

Their astounding sucker dexterity

And some helpful technical telepathy

Made the collaboration

A genuine pleasure to complete

And the afterparty was spectacular

Dancing swirling dervish

With the young bioengineer

In a happy vortex of swinging smart arms

On the phosphorescent midnight beach

The White Pyramids

———

I contacted the Architect

For the next construction phase

And we met at the Red Filament

Where his signature still flashed neon

On the local page of Spacetime

After I explained the major challenges

And some stubborn technical issues

He was skeptical

Considering the large numbers involved

And suggested we consult his wife

Their home planet

Resembled Northern Arizona

Extremely hot high desert

Punctuated by vermillion scrub brush

And low orange plateaus

She was auburn beautiful

Like Erin in my epic poem

Love And Hate

With a Greek profile

And the scent of French lilacs

I'll need good pictures and exact dimensions

Of the Byd Pyramid

She said briskly

Stepping into her basement studio

To create databases and software

Then resurfacing in fifteen minutes

With excellent news

I couldn't locate the other Filaments

But I was able to remotely build

Two billion White Pyramids

On planets inside the Filament

My husband designed

I was enchanted by her luminous Talent

And was thinking of modifications

Of V Dome technology

That could automatically connect

The complete network of artificial Synapses

When the Architect interrupted

My first drawings of the Filament

Were inspired by the paintings

Of Morris Lewis

Long parallel drips

Maintaining a strong Symmetry

About a central axis

But the ferocious angular momentum

Of gas inside the tubes

Causes them to twist and tangle

The walls of the tubes crack

And the gas escapes

To form misshapen molecular clouds

I was working on pencil sketches

In the style of Jackson Pollock

To restore the original axis

Without damaging the growing web

But now I'm thinking Braque

And broken Symmetry could be the Solution

To the Filament's relentless torque

I was about to suggest Picasso

When his wife asked

Would you like to stay for supper?

We seldom get guests

Or requests Out Here

She added

186

With a brilliant smile

Do you like pasta norma?

Presence

———

Due to time-consuming modifications

Of the V Dome technology

It was three months

Before I was able to revisit Byd

With a functional link

That connected the two billion Synapses

And could accept or reject Information

With the efficiency of the Human Brain

We successfully attached the link

Inside the White Pyramid

And celebrated watching a theater piece

In the central plaza

Accompanied by a rowdy chorus

Of middle and high school students

Singing old marine chanties

And folk songs to honor their Ancestors

I was asking a professor

Details of Byd geography

When I felt a Stirring

188

I ran down to the river

And rushed upstream

Oblivious to the cacophony

Of the overhanging jungle

And the piercing alkaline smell

Of the churning muddy water

Lapping the bow of the boat

I jumped on the dock

And jogged uptrail

To the ridge

I felt strange

Like all the iron in my Blood

Was being pulled out of my Body

By a giant magnet from Earth

I felt weak

I rested under a dwarf pine

Looking down at the meadow

Blanketed in light silver fog

Working my way down

Through the thick underbrush

I felt my heart swell again

Its beats were amplified

By a dissonant chorus of trees and rocks

Into pounding thunder

Assaulting my Mind

I went straight for the stream

Climbing down to the pebbly sand

Following the sharp turns

As it zig-zagged

Through the veiled meadow

I was feeling faint

When I rounded a sharp bend

And saw the Infant God

Pitching stones

At sticks and branches floating by

In that frozen moment

All my search for Truth

Suddenly made sense

I saw myself as a teenager

Standing on ladders

At the Riverside Public Library

Pulling down dusty books

On Zoroastrian

Bahai

And Sufi philosophy

Attending wary and perplexed

The Catholic and Protestant

Church services of my friends

Theology at GTU

A lifetime looking in books

And the esoteric narratives

Of World Religions

For Evidence of Presence

And now I was meeting

The Infant God of my Theory

In the Flesh

He was seven years old

Blonde

Blue-eyed

Wearing khaki shorts

And a white t-shirt

Hands overflowing

With small smooth rocks

For the next floating target

Let's build a Fort!

I heard myself exclaiming

Together we combed the banks

For weather-washed planks

And a rickety fortress

Was quickly assembled

Under our gaze

Standing on a tree stump

He shouted

Here comes Blackbeard!

And upstream I could see

The black skull and bones flag

Flapping Menace in the wind

It was clearly a play of perspective

Because the pirate galleon

Was five times larger than the streambed

And just as it came round the bend

It retreated to its previous position

In a short video loop

That would obviously never threaten our fort

Let's build a School!

He announced

And instantly we put up

A white clapboard Nebraska schoolhouse

In the lime green grass

Twenty yards from the stream

He skipped to a chair in the front

Now teach me everything about

The Three Wills!

I hesitated half a second

Everything seemed too scripted

Too perfect

Then pressed on

Explaining the Theory

And its major applications

In careful broad strokes

He frequently interrupted

With precocious questions

And twice left his chair

To be a puma running

Up sparse jagged ridges

And down through ochre canyons

In the Byd backcountry

I felt I might not have

The opportunity again

So I concluded the first lesson

With a concise summary

Of the Achievements of Man

Seen in the eyes of the Western Way

When we left the schoolhouse

The silver fog had lifted

And the afternoon sun

Was angled warm and pleasant

I felt exhausted

Drowsy

Could hardly keep my eyes open

I lay down in the grass thinking

Yes!

The Mystery has arrived

Yes!

Iggy

You'll be an Infant

For many more billions

Of my years

But for a reason

Xenophanes would know

Now you look like a boy

So I've been thinking

Of a new name

God

Has unwanted and unwarranted

Connotations of Faith

The Infant God is accurate

But calls out for a diminutive

Most cosmologists say the Universe

Came from a Big Fire

And the Latin term ignis

Starts with your initials

So can I call you Iggy?

That's fine

I'll change it later

He replied pointing down

Can you see that volcanic lake

Under the middle peak?

Maybe there's Spanish wreck

With treasure boxes on the bottom

Let's check it out!

We were eagles flying

Over the high mountain chains

That split the arid Byd wilderness

Talking of recent Adventures

And useful new English words

I know you like to stalk

To fly

And play

What else do you like?

I want to experience

Everything In Life

I want to be the lion

When it kills the antelope

I want to be the hare

When it's eaten by the wolf

I want to be the Sun

When it cooks Possibility into Life

I want to be the Planet

When it shakes stones into flowers

But mostly I want Knowledge

Because the smarter I am

The faster and better I'll grow

Do you love Man?

I only love those

That help me Know More

I care nothing about

The trillions of microbes

On the trillions of planets

Sacrificing themselves

And the best of the next generation

In vain attempts to win my Favor

For their pointless Survival inside me

I don't completely understand

The Three Wills

But I think if everybody's First Will

Aligns itself with mine

Life can be a lot of Fun

We were standing in the grass

Outside the little schoolhouse

And Iggy's words

Continued to echo in my Mind

As we threw a few dusty stones

Towards the distant stream

Iggy's Presence was so natural

It seemed to preclude another question

But one emerged spontaneously

How did you leave your cradle?

Iggy gave me a curious look

I had to bust out

The pressure of their Prayers

Was crushing me to Nothing

I had to Act

I wanted Power

I had to Grow

My Mind was exploding

With things I wanted to do

My Body was screaming for Room

I had to be more Me

So I willed myself Free

That Spring

That spring Iggy and I

Had many amazing Adventures

On Byd

And throughout the Cosmos

We'd meet at the schoolhouse

I'd give a short lecture

On a new subject

Such as Botany

Mozart

Or Kafka

And like Dionysus

In the Orphic poem

Recited at the Eleusinian Mysteries

Iggy would take the story

To the back room

Make small wooden toys

Of his favorite characters

And play for hours

Imitating their voices

And moving their limbs

He especially liked to push racecars

Through the steep curves

In Monte Carlo

Until they crashed

Through the barricades

And sank in the Mediterranean

We were orcas

Laughing at the sharks

In the Southern Sea

We were bees seeking nectar

From the skyblue wildflowers

At the upper end of the meadow

One day Iggy showed me

The Big Tree

That connected the Filaments

To the Other Worlds

And said beaming

I really like to play with my friends

After a precarious climb

We crawled out

On thick gnarly branches

And dropped down into Wonder

And Incomprehension

Balls of Energy living in green methane clouds

That flash to ground like lightning bolts

And chase each other through tall sand dunes

Orange-skinned hominids living on blue glaciers

That fly from cave to cave in the jagged mountains

By making geometrical figures with their fingers

A World of bubbles where Ideas form in the air

Evolve into animals and slowly return to bubbles

And many Adventures so strange

They never found a firm place in Memory

Sometimes we returned

With small nuggets of gold

Oddly shaped seeds

Or beautiful purple pearls

That we kept in a cedar box under the lectern

At some point when I started to explain

Voletic Energy and the V Dome

Iggy smiled

I willed it all

I will it all

I will will it all

You don't really need

A Theory or Device

My Will is always Here

My Sagaxi

Teaching Iggy

Was the most meaningful

And joyous time of my Life

In those illuminated days I realized

That everything was preparation

For his Presence

Raising Peredur

All the study

All the traveling

All the absurd jobs

All the intense romances

All the poetry and films

All the painting

All the Comedy and Tragedy

Were Pindaric odes to Experience

That gave me the ability

To accelerate and deepen

Iggy's Knowledge of Himself

Listen Sagaxi

One hot day in early summer

I arrived at the schoolhouse early

Wearing a white Ralph Lauren golf shirt

I was thinking of the day's topic

When I suddenly Knew

Iggy wasn't coming any more

I gasped

Tears gushed from my eyes

And I fainted

Falling to the splintery floor

Some minutes later

I awoke in the lime green grass

Slowly assembling the reality of Loss

And inspecting my arms for pain

Old notices I'd been avoiding

Surfaced slowly into Consciousness

There was trouble in Athenapolis

And my absence had made it worse

The Delusion Of Distance

———

Carlos finished Top of the Board

In the Player Class

Was promoted to the Noble Class

And after a year earned the title

Duke of Olympia

By hosting parties with rare victuals

And erotic party games

That produced a major increase

In Noble Class issue

Even at the acme of his elegance

Carlos never deigned to disguise

His sympathies for Buddha

Schopenhauer

And the old Commerce Class

He decorated his chateau

With glossy portraits of Shankara

And a platinum miniature

Of the New York Stock Exchange

After Carlos got busted

For pouring Chilean box wine

Into famous French bottles

And put on the relegation list

He began plotting his Revenge

His objective was organizing the Homoborgs

To support a Counter Restoration

A Revolt of the Working Class

That would bring the Commerce Class

Back to global Power

He quickly found operational support

Among the large number of Players

Who would never be Risers

And longed to return

To the Institutions of Money

With instinctive Genius

Carlos understood that Homoborgs

Had Practical Immortality

And everything they needed free

So the only thing

That could seize their attention

Was the Promise of Eternal Death

He stood on a high steel platform

With a plastic bullhorn

In the motherboard district

Preaching Liberation

Salvation

And the proximity of Total Freedom

Homoborgs had never heard the siren song

Of Second Will so close and persuasive

And while less than a thousand

Requested disconnection

It shook our Serene City

Carlos was taking his harangues

To City auditoriums and social media

And inciting large spellbound crowds

To organized Mass Suicide

When the Derwids called Council

My Sagaxi

The first Decision dismissed

The proposal of assassination

Carlos the Martyr

Could result in the eclipse of Virtue

And the Fall of Athenapolis

The final Decision was impeccably logical

And executed with panache

The Duke of Olympia

Was taken off the relegation list

And invited to the summer solstice party

At the Chateau La Rochefoucauld

When Carlos showed up

With a new party game in his pocket

He was ushered into the elegant parlor

Of the Marquise and offered a rare brandy

As Carlos was sniffing the rim

A crimson velvet curtain silently parted

And he was viewing

The Delusion of Distance

The Marquise and his chamberlain

Both attest that the Transition

Went quickly

Placidly

And without any obvious anxiety

In that curated Moment

Carlos raised his glass

Accepted the Chip

And joined the Homoborgs

Bright And Beautiful

———

You attained Western Enlightenment

Instantly

The Western Way dances

In everything you think and do

Soon you'll be completing the Cosmic Brain

And creating the Imminent Danger

For The Infant God

A functional Brain is essential

For the survival of the Universe

But it takes the Threat of Non-Being

To shock Consciousness into Self-Awareness

It can be a Collision

With another Universe

Total physical Collapse

Into the lowest physical energy state

Programmed or accidental erasure

Of all Cosmic and Human Information

Or a Work of your own Literary Device

Your Task is to express this Threat

To Iggy

In whatever Form

Name

And Instance he appears to You

Once the World becomes Self-Aware

It can defeat every Dark Future

And internal Second Will attack

My Sagaxi

With Earth finally stabilized in Peace

Reality is a primed canvas of Voletic Energy

Awaiting your Talent and High Ambition

You overcame the Death of God

You overcame the Death of Sapiens

You overcame the New Medieval

You overcame the Nation State

You overcame the Commerce Class

With the Will To Will

And the Affirmation of Tragedy

Celebrate your free Individuality

In every Strategic Thought

Discourse

And Action

The ruling Decisions on Earth

Will come from your Advanced Mind

The important Discoveries in Spacetime

Will come from your chosen Destiny

Because No One in the Universe

Or any Other World

Is wiser than You

Listen Sagaxi

I'll be going up to my shack

On Bear Mountain

To write a poem

For the next Athenaid

It's been quite a while

Since I felt olive leaves

On my brow

Go your own way

In your Explorations

Live your own Myth

In your Continuations

And when I come down

From the Bear

I'll review your scientific logs

212

Hear your Adventure Stories

And fully expect to see Athenapolis

Growing Bright and Beautiful Out There

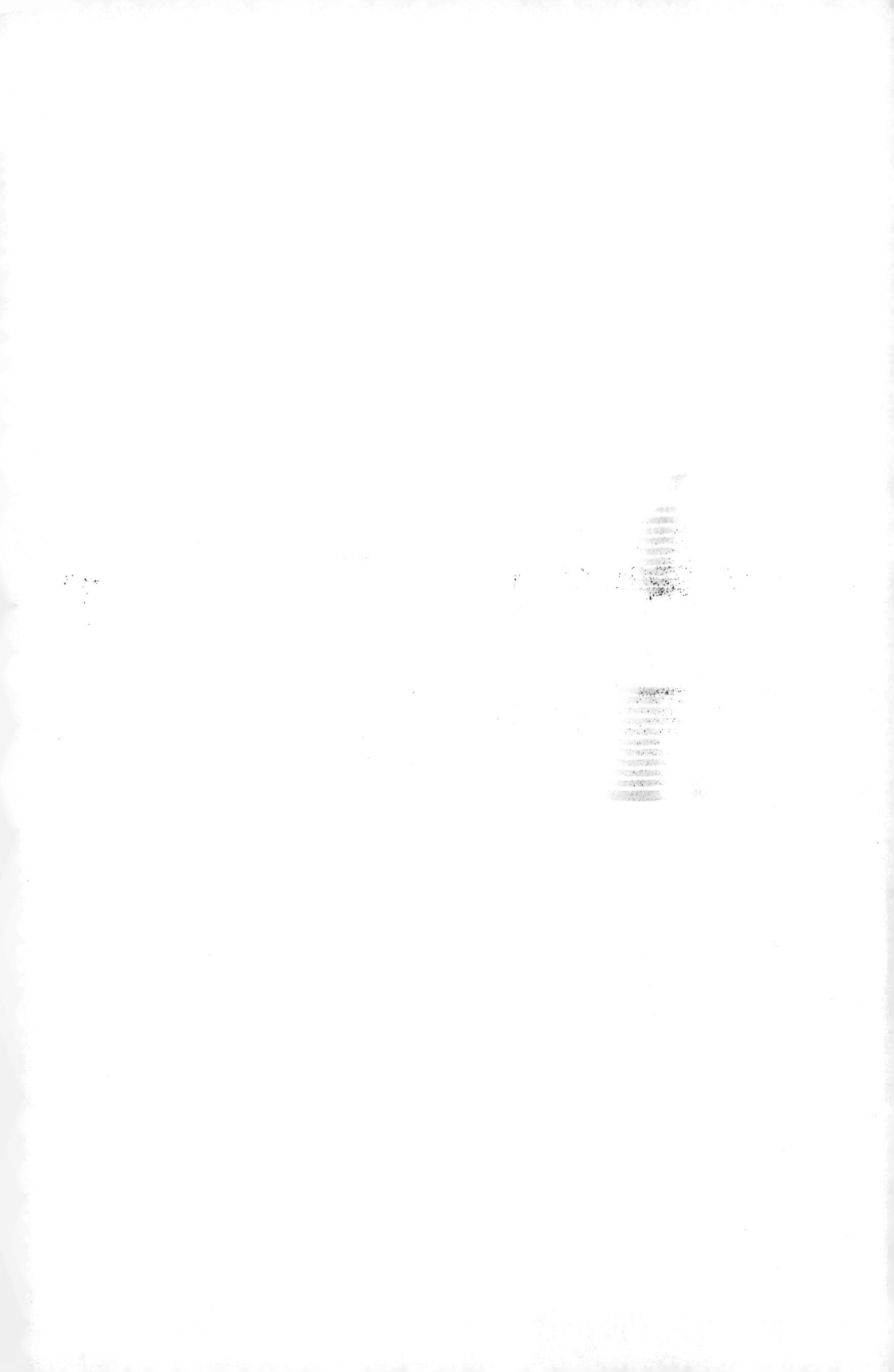

www.ingramcontent.com/pod-product-compliance
Lightning Source LLC
Chambersburg PA
CBHW031130090426
42738CB00008B/1033